Typing Time

JACK P. HOGGATT, ED.D.
Professor of Business Communication
University of Wisconsin
Eau Claire (WI)

JON A. SHANK, ED.D.
Professor of Education
Robert Morris University
Moon Township (PA)

SOUTH-WESTERN
★ ™
THOMSON LEARNING

Australia • Canada • Mexico • Singapore • Spain • United Kingdom • United States

SOUTH-WESTERN ✦ THOMSON LEARNING

Typing Time
Jack Hoggatt, Jon Shank

Editor-in-Chief:
Jack Calhoun

Vice President/ Executive Publisher:
Dave Shaut

Team Leader:
Karen Schmohe

Acquisitions Editor:
Jane Congdon

Technology Project Manager:
Gayle Statman

Executive Marketing Manager:
Carol Volz

Channel Manager:
Nancy Long

Marketing Coordinator:
Cira Brown

Editor:
Kim Kusnerak

Consulting Developmental Editor:
Dianne S. Rankin

Production Manager:
Tricia Boies

Manufacturing Coordinator:
Charlene Taylor

Compositor:
Cover to Cover Publishing, Inc.

Printer:
Quebecor World
Dubuque, IA

Design Project Manager:
Stacy Jenkins Shirley

Cover/Internal Designer:
Ann Small, a small design studio

Cover Illustration:
Julie Baker

Permissions Editor:
Linda Ellis

CONTENTS

Preface vi

Welcome to Typing Time vii

LESSONS 1-20	ALPHABET	

LESSON 1	Home Keys (fdsa jkl;)	1
2	Review Home Keys (fdsa jkl;)	4
3	e and h	6
4	o and r	8
5	Review	10
6	i and t	12
7	Left Shift and period (.)	14
8	u and c	17
9	Review	19
10	n and w	22
11	g and Right Shift	24
12	b and p	26
13	Review	28
14	m and x	31
15	y and z	33
16	q and comma (,)	35
17	Review	38
18	v and colon (:)	40
19	CAPS LOCK and question mark (?)	42
20	Tab	45

SKILL BUILDERS 1-5	

SKILL BUILDER 1	. . . .	48
2	. . . .	50
3	. . . .	52
4	. . . .	54
5	. . . .	56

LESSON 21 Keyboarding Enrichment and Review 1 and 7. 58

22 Keyboarding Enrichment and Review 4 and 8. 60

23 Keyboarding Enrichment and Review 5 and 9. 63

24 Keyboarding Enrichment and Review 3 and 0. 66

25 Keyboarding Enrichment and Review 2 and 6. 68

26 Keyboarding Enrichment and Review 0 to 9. 71

27 Keyboarding Enrichment and Review / and $ 74

28 Keyboarding Enrichment and Review % and - 76

29 Keyboarding Enrichment and Review # and & 79

30 Keyboarding Enrichment and Review (and) 82

31 Keyboarding Enrichment and Review ' and " 85

32 Keyboarding Enrichment and Review _ and * 88

33 Keyboarding Enrichment and Review @ and + ... 91

34 Keyboarding Enrichment and Review ! and \ 95

35 Keyboarding Enrichment and Review =, [, and] 98

36 Keyboarding Enrichment and Review > and < 101

37 Keyboarding Enrichment and Reports 104

38 Keyboarding Enrichment and Reports 109

39 Keyboarding Enrichment and Reports 112

40 Keyboarding Enrichment and Reports 115

Index I-1

Expect More from South-Western, and Get It!

Typing Time software is a new addition to the incredibly successful line of South-Western keyboarding software. Learning to type properly is critical for younger students. *Typing Time* combines the latest technology with a superior and time-tested method of instruction to provide an all-in-one program covering letter keys, numbers and symbols, and numeric keypad basics. Through the effective use of animation, movies, and skillbuilding games, *Typing Time* teaches correct finger placement, builds basic skills, then works on speed and accuracy.

> Windows CD and User Guide (Network/Site License) 0-538-69990-6
>
> Macintosh CD and User Guide (Network/Site License) 0-538-43440-6

Skillbusters: Mystery at Wellsley Manor is an interactive mystery game that builds keyboarding speed and accuracy. In this software program, clues surface only after students achieve keyboarding goals. Available for Windows and Macintosh, *Skillbusters* can be used after students have learned the keys and need some incentive to build skill and accuracy. (10+ hours)

> Windows/Macintosh CD (Network/Site License). 0-538-68343-0

Integrated Computer Projects is an ideal source of computer literacy projects for students in Grades 6-8 who already have some basic software skills. It includes basic, intermediate, and advanced projects covering word processing, spreadsheet, database, presentation, and Internet skills. Students develop critical-thinking and decision-making skills while writing a story, planning a budget, making a presentation, shopping for a computer, solving a mystery, and completing other computer activities. (30+ hours)

> Text (softcover, 2-color, 192 pages) 0-538-43386-8

CyberStopMedia.com is a non-software-specific integrated applications simulation. As employees of a cyber business that sells CDs and DVDs, students use intermediate to advanced word processing, voice technology, spreadsheet, database, desktop publishing, and telecommunications skills to complete their tasks. (30+ hours)

> Text/CD Package (hardcover, top spiral, 2-color, 96 pages) 0-538-72439-0

Digitacion para el dominio de la computadora (Spanish version of *Keyboarding for Computer Success*) is designed for the user who wants to learn basic keyboarding, but is more comfortable reading Spanish. All instructions are written in Spanish, allowing the user to focus on keyboarding rather than language translation. The lessons, skill checks, and assessment exercises are in English. (25+ hours)

> Text (softcover, top spiral, 4-color, 112 pages) 0-538-69863-2

SOUTH-WESTERN
THOMSON LEARNING

Join us on the Internet at www.swep.com

PREFACE

Typing Time is a textbook that correlates with and reinforces the lessons in the *Typing Time* software program. With the *Typing Time* software, students use the computer to learn alphabetic and numeric keyboarding and the number keypad.

The lessons in *Typing Time* reinforce the alphabetic, number, and symbol key reaches in the same sequence as presented in the *Typing Time* software program. After the home row keys are reviewed in Lessons 1 and 2, each lesson that follows reinforces two new keys. Review lessons begin with Lesson 5 and are included every fourth lesson thereafter. Students should complete the corresponding software lesson prior to completing a textbook lesson.

In addition to reinforcing key reaches, the textbook goes beyond the *Typing Time* software to provide word processing, research and composition, grammar, and report production activities. These activities not only provide variety in the lessons, but also focus on many of the skills suggested by the *Secretary's Commission on Achieving Necessary Skills* (SCANS) report.

The *Typing Time* textbook, used in conjunction with the *Typing Time* software, gives students a comprehensive learning program. Using this program, students can master basic keyboarding, word processing, and report production skills while improving grammar, research, composition, and thinking skills.

About The Authors

Dr. Jon A. Shank is a Professor of Education at Robert Morris University in Moon Township, Pennsylvania. For more than 20 years, he served as Dean of the School of Applied Sciences and Education at Robert Morris. Dr. Shank retired as Dean in 1998 to return to full-time teaching. He currently teaches methods courses to students who are studying to become business educators. Dr. Shank holds memberships in regional, state, and national business education organizations. He has received many honors during his career, including Outstanding Post-Secondary Business Educator in Pennsylvania.

Dr. Jack P. Hoggatt is Department Chair for the Department of Business Communications at the University of Wisconsin-Eau Clair. He has taught courses in Business Writing, Advanced Business Communications, and the communication component of the university's Master in Business Administration (MBA) program. Dr. Hoggatt has held offices in a number of professional organizations and has been the recipient of the Outstanding Post-Secondary Business Educator Award in Wisconsin. He has served as an advisor to local and state business organizations. Dr. Hoggatt is involved with his community and the school activities of his four children.

Welcome to Typing Time

With the *Typing Time* software, you can use the power of your computer to learn alphabetic and numeric keyboarding and the keypad. The lessons in the *Typing Time* textbook correlate with and reinforce the software lessons. Follow your teacher's instructions regarding when to complete the software and textbook lessons.

START TYPING TIME SOFTWARE

Your computer should be turned on with the operating system window displayed.

Windows

1. Click the *Start* button.
2. Point to the Programs menu; a submenu displays listing programs.
3. Click *South-Western Keyboarding* and then click *Typing Time*.
4. The *Typing Time* Log In dialog box appears.

Macintosh

1. Double-click the *Typing Time* icon.
2. The *Typing Time* Log In dialog box appears.

LOG IN PROCEDURE

LOG IN TIP
To view only the names in your class, click the down arrow for the Class ID drop-down list. Click the name of your class.

1. On the Log In dialog box, click your name in the list at the left. (When using the program for the first time, you must complete the new student registration as described on the next page.)
2. Click *OK*.
3. Enter your password and click *OK*.
4. After you log in, the *Typing Time* main screen appears.

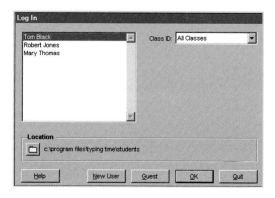

NEW STUDENT REGISTRATION

1. The first time you use *Typing Time*, click *New User* on the Log In box to register.

2. In the New Student dialog box, enter your name in the First name and Last name boxes.
3. Enter a Class ID such as the name of your class or other ID provided by your teacher.
4. Enter a password. Write the password on a piece of paper and store it in a safe place.
5. A data path, such as **c:\program files\typing time\students,** may already be set. If your teacher instructs you to store files in a different folder, you must set the path accordingly. Click the *Data Path* button to browse through the directories to locate a folder where you are to store files.
6. Click OK to complete the registration process. The *Typing Time* main screen appears.

MAIN SCREEN

The *Typing Time* main screen provides a menu from which you may select keyboarding or keypad lessons and skill-building lessons. Games, movies, and 3-D animation showing proper keying techniques may also be accessed from the menu. Buttons that allow you to access the Log In dialog box, the program Help feature, the Word Processor, and to Exit the program appear to the left of the menu.

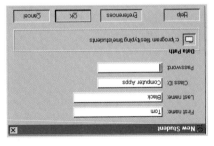

LESSON 1

Home Keys (fdsa jkl;)

© Photo by Erik Snobeck/Digital Imaging Group

TECHNIQUE TIP

Place the keyboard directly in front of your chair with the front edge of the keyboard even with the edge of the desk. Place your book to the right of the keyboard with the top raised for easy reading.

WORD PROCESSING

WORD PROCESSOR FEATURE

Key and save lessons from this textbook by using Typing Time's *Word Processor feature.*

Access the Word Processor

1. Start the *Typing Time* program.

2. Complete the Log In procedure.

3. When the *Typing Time* main screen appears, click the *Word Processor* button. The Word Processor screen appears.

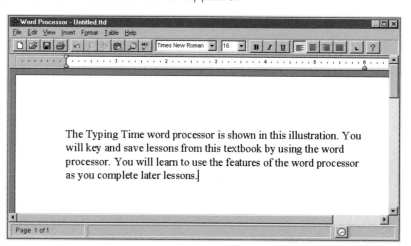

GRAMMAR CORNER

Study the spelling and definitions of the words below. Key the Learn line, noting the word choices. Key the Apply lines, selecting the correct words.

affect (verb) influence; produce an effect upon
effect (noun) result

LEARN 1 Prices can **affect** sales and have an **effect** on profits.
APPLY 2 His school spirit had an (affect, effect) on Jane.
APPLY 3 Practice (affects, effects) how we play the game.

© PhotoDisc, Inc.

WRITING CORNER

Open a new file and create a report. Using Copy/Paste, insert text from the following files that you created earlier as the report body: **Composers**, **Baseball**, **Artists**, **Movie Stars**, **Inventors**, and **Musicians**.

Key **FAMOUS PEOPLE** as the report title. Use the famous person's name from each file as a side heading that precedes the information about that person. Compose a short introductory paragraph and key it between the report title and the first side heading. Format the text as a report and number all pages except page 1.

Prepare a title page using the report title, your name, your school name, and the current date. Save the document as **L40Report2**.

Key each line as shown below. Keep your eyes on the textbook as you key. (Do not key line numbers.)

Practice Home Keys

1 f ff j jj d dd k kk s ss l ll a aa ; ;; fdsa jkl;
2 f ff j jj d dd k kk s ss l ll a aa ; ;; fdsa jkl;

3 a aa ; ;; s ss l ll d dd k kk f ff j jj fjdk sla;
4 a aa ; ;; s ss l ll d dd k kk f ff j jj fjdk sla;

5 a;a sls dkd fjf ;a; lsl kdk jfj asdf jkl; a;sl fj
6 a;a sls dkd fjf ;a; lsl kdk jfj asdf jkl; a;sl fj

7 a a as as ad ad ask ask lad lad fad fad jak jak j
8 a a as as ad ad ask ask lad lad fad fad jak jak j

9 all all fad fad jak jak add add ask ask ads ads a
10 all all fad fad jak jak add add ask ask ads ads a

11 a kaka; as all; ask dad; all ads; ask all; a lad;
12 a kaka; as all; ask dad; all ads; ask all; a lad;

GRAMMAR CORNER

Study the definitions of the words below and the Learn lines. Note the correct way to use the words. Compose one sentence (in longhand) using the word "its" and another sentence using the word "it's."

its (adjective) of or relating to itself as the possessor
it's (contraction) it is; it has

LEARN 1 The dog bit **its** tail.
LEARN 2 The dog will have **its** shot this week.
LEARN 3 The dog is tired; **it's** resting by the tree.
LEARN 4 Because the box is filled with books, **it's** very heavy.

The lakes vary greatly in elevation. Lake Superior, the highest, lies 600 feet (183 meters) above sea level, while Lake Ontario, the lowest, lies just 245 feet (75 meters) above sea level. There is a 325-foot difference in elevation between lakes Erie and Ontario. Most of the water from the lakes drains into the St. Lawrence River, which flows into the Atlantic Ocean (<u>The World Almanac and Book of Facts</u>, 1999). The depth of the Great Lakes varies greatly too. The deepest, Lake Superior, is 1,333 feet (406 meters) deep. Lake Erie, the shallowest, is only 210 feet (64 meters) deep (<u>The Information Please Almanac</u>, 1994).

<u>Connecting Waterways</u>

Three sets of locks and canals make it possible for ships to sail from one Great Lake to another and from Lake Ontario to the Atlantic Ocean, from which they can sail to any port in the world. The canals and the bodies of water they connect are listed here.

1. Welland Canal--connects Lake Erie and Lake Ontario.
2. Soo Canal--connects Lake Superior and Lake Huron.
3. St. Lawrence Seaway--connects Lake Ontario with the Atlantic Ocean.

<u>Significance of the Lakes</u>

The five Great Lakes and the canals that link them together make up the most important inland waterway in North America. They provide the inexpensive transportation system needed to make the Great Lakes region one of the most important industrial areas in the United States.

REFERENCES

<u>The Information Please Almanac</u>. "Large Lakes of the World." Boston: Houghton Mifflin Company, 1994.

<u>The World Almanac and Book of Facts</u>. "Major Natural Lakes of the World." Mahwah, NJ: World Almanac Books, 1999.

<u>The World Book Encyclopedia</u>. "Great Lakes." Chicago: World Book, Inc., 1993.

WORD PROCESSING

PROGRAM COMMANDS

Choose program commands and options by using menus and the toolbar. Click a menu name on the Menu bar to display a pull-down menu of commands, features, and options. The Save command is highlighted on the File pull-down menu. Saving a document allows you to exit the program without losing the text you have keyed.

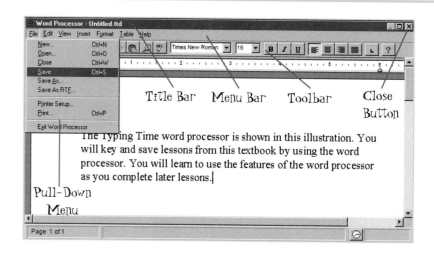

The Typing Time word processor is shown in this illustration. You will key and save lessons from this textbook by using the word processor. You will learn to use the features of the word processor as you complete later lessons.

COMPUTER WIZ

Click the *Save* button on the toolbar to access the Save As dialog box quickly.

SAVE DOCUMENT AND EXIT WORD PROCESSOR

1. Click *File* on the Menu bar. Click *Save*.

2. The Save As dialog box appears.

3. Key the filename (**Lesson1** for this file) in the File name text box and click *Save*.

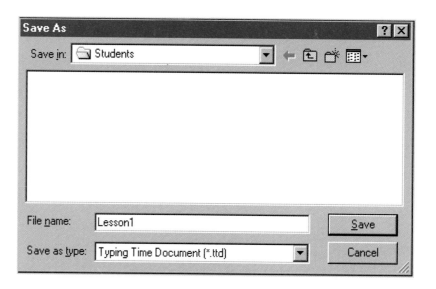

4. To exit the Word Processor, click *File* on the Menu bar and click *Exit Word Processor*. You can also exit the program by clicking the *Close* button in the upper-right corner of the Word Processor window.

Two-Page Report with Textual Citations and References

1. Key the information below as a report. Number all pages except page 1. Place the references on a separate page. Spell check and proofread carefully. Correct all errors. Save the document as **L40Report1**.

2. Open a new document. Prepare a title page using the report title, your name, your school name, and the current date. Save the title page as **L40Title**.

THE GREAT LAKES

The five Great Lakes are the largest group of fresh-water lakes in the world, and they make up the most important inland waterway in North America. The lakes formed more than 250,000 years ago during the Ice Age.

> A glacier moved south across the land of what is now the Great Lakes region. The glacier dug out deep depressions in the soft rocks of the region and picked up great amounts of earth and rocks. The glacier withdrew from 11,000 to 15,000 years ago, and the earth and rocks blocked the natural drainage of the depressions. Water from the melting glacier gradually filled in the depressions and formed the Great Lakes. (<u>World Book Encyclopedia</u>, 1993)

<u>Physical Features</u>

Although the Great Lakes (Lake Erie, Lake Huron, Lake Michigan, Lake Ontario, and Lake Superior) were all formed by glacial activity during the same period, they are quite different from one another. The irregular movement of the glacier created variation in the size, elevation, and depth of the lakes.

The Great Lakes have a combined area of 94,510 square miles (244,780 square kilometers). Lake Superior, the largest of the lakes, is only slightly smaller than Maine; and Lake Ontario, the smallest of the lakes, is about the size of New Jersey.

(continued on next page)

LESSON 2

Review Home Keys (fdsa jkl;)

PRACTICE MAKES PERFECT

Key each line as shown below. After keying the lines, save the document using **Lesson2** for the filename. Then exit the Word Processor.

Practice Home Keys

1 ask dad; ask dad; a sad lad; a sad lad; a sad lass
2 ask dad; ask dad; a sad lad; a sad lad; a sad lass

DS

3 as a fall; as a fall; ask a sad lad; ask a sad lad
4 as a fall; as a fall; ask a sad lad; ask a sad lad

DS

5 a fall; a fall; as a jak; as a jak; as dad; as dad
6 a fall; a fall; as a jak; as a jak; as dad; as dad

GRAMMAR CORNER

Read the capitalization rules below. Study the Learn sentences and note how the rules are applied. Compose one sentence (in longhand) for each rule, applying the rule.

Capitalize the first word of a sentence.

LEARN 1 The men came to work late today.

LEARN 2 They will not be able to meet the deadline.

Capitalize names of people. Capitalize a personal title when it precedes a name.

LEARN 3 I read Mr. Johnson's letter yesterday.

LEARN 4 I have an appointment with Dr. Joseph Ryan this afternoon.

LESSON 40

Keyboarding Enrichment and Reports

Key each line twice SS (once slowly, then again at a faster pace). DS between 2-line groups.

1 Gadwin Zan will buy the exquisite jacket from the shop.
2 Order 35791 was replaced with Order 46802 on August 12.
3 To my dismay, the girls kept the big dog in the kennel.

PRACTICE MAKES PERFECT

Set the Timer for 1 minute. Key at least two 1' timings on each paragraph. Then key two 2' writings on both paragraphs. Determine *gwam* and errors.

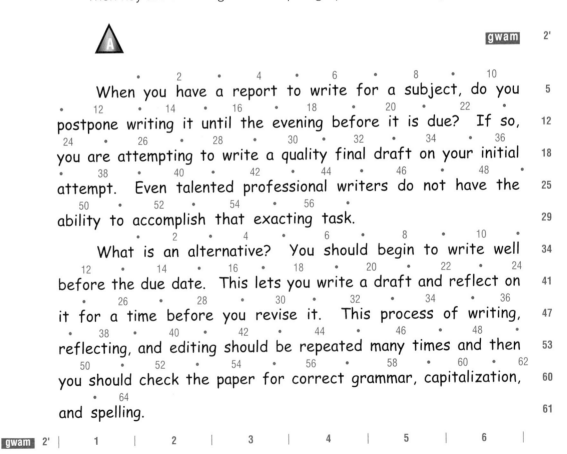

| | gwam | 2' |

A

```
         •    2    •    4    •    6    •    8    •   10
    When you have a report to write for a subject, do you       5
  •   12    •   14    •   16    •   18    •   20    •   22    •
postpone writing it until the evening before it is due?  If so,   12
  24    •   26    •   28    •   30    •   32    •   34    •   36
you are attempting to write a quality final draft on your initial   18
  •   38    •   40    •   42    •   44    •   46    •   48    •
attempt.  Even talented professional writers do not have the    25
  50    •   52    •   54    •   56    •
ability to accomplish that exacting task.                       29
         •    2    •    4    •    6    •    8    •   10    •
    What is an alternative?  You should begin to write well     34
  12    •   14    •   16    •   18    •   20    •   22    •   24
before the due date.  This lets you write a draft and reflect on   41
  •   26    •   28    •   30    •   32    •   34    •   36
it for a time before you revise it.  This process of writing,   47
  •   38    •   40    •   42    •   44    •   46    •   48    •
reflecting, and editing should be repeated many times and then   53
  50    •   52    •   54    •   56    •   58    •   60    •   62
you should check the paper for correct grammar, capitalization,   60
  •   64
and spelling.                                                   61
```

gwam 2' | 1 | 2 | 3 | 4 | 5 | 6 |

OPEN COMMAND

The Open command is an option on the File menu. Use it to open a document you saved earlier.

Click the *Open* button on the toolbar to access the Open dialog box quickly.

Open Document

1. Click *File* on the Menu bar. Click *Open*. The Open dialog box appears.
2. Click the filename. It will appear in the File name box. Click *Open*.

KEYING ON YOUR OWN: HOME KEYS

Access the Word Processor and open **Lesson2**. Beginning a DS below the last line, key the lines shown below. Key each line twice SS; DS between 2-line groups.

1   as a lad asks; as a lad asks; add a fad; add a fad
                                                            DS
2   ask a lass; ask a lass; all fall ads; all fall ads
                                                            DS
3   all fall; all fall; a sad dad asks; a sad dad asks

WORD PROCESSING

SAVE AS COMMAND

The Save As command is an option on the File menu. Use it to save a document under a new name—the original file remains unchanged. The file created using this command contains the original document with the changes made to the document.

Save a Document with a New Name

1. With a document open, click *File* on the Menu bar. Click *Save As*. The Save As dialog box appears.
2. Key the new filename in the File name box. Click *Save*.

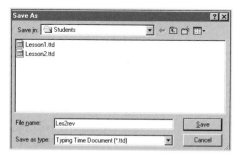

TECH TALK

New Command: Opens a new blank document. Click *File* on the menu bar and click *New* to open a new document.

Practice What You Have Learned

1. Save **Lesson2** as **Les2rev**.
2. Open a new document by clicking the *New* button on the toolbar.
3. Exit the Word Processor.

1. Open **L37Header1**.
2. Print page 3.
3. Open **L37Header2**.
4. Print pages 2 and 3.

WORD PROCESSING
APPLY WHAT YOU HAVE LEARNED

Reports with Textual Citations and References

Study the information in the report below. Key the report following the formatting guides. Make corrections as marked. Place the references on a separate page and number all pages except page 1. (Review hanging indent on p. 93.) Spell check and proofread the document. Correct all errors. Save the document as **L39Report**.

REPORT WITH TEXTUAL CITATIONS

Footnotes, endnotes, or textual citations can be used to give credit for quoted or paraphrased material. This report explains how to include textual citations and a separate reference list within a report.

TEXTUAL Citations

Textual citations are keyed in parentheses in the report body. These citations include the name (s) of the author (s), year of publication, and page number (s) of the reference material. Quotations of up to three keyed lines are enclosed in quotation marks. Quotations (four or more keyed lines) are left indented. Paraphrased material is not enclosed in quotation marks (Hoggatt, Shank, and Robinson, 2002, 70).

Reference List

All references used in a formal report are listed at the end under the heading references. QS between the heading and first reference. References are listed alphabetically by authors' last names. SS each reference; DS between references. Begin the first line of each reference at the left margin; indent other lines 0.5". If the reference list appears on the last page of the report body, QS before the heading, REFERENCES. If the list appears on a separate page, use the same margins as for the first page of the report and include a page number (Robinson, et al., 2000, 144).

References

Hoggatt, Jack P., Jon A. Shank, and Jerry W. Robinson. _Century 21 Computer Applications & Keyboarding_. 7th ed. Cincinnati: South-Western Educational Publishing, 2002.

Robinson, Jerry W., et al. _Century 21 Keyboarding & Information Processing_. 6th ed. Cincinnati: South-Western Educational Publishing, 2000.

LESSON 3

e and h

CASEY'S WARM UP

Key each line twice single-spaced (SS): once slowly, then again at a faster pace. Double-space (DS) between 2-line groups. Save the document using **Lesson3** for the filename.

1 al ks ja fl ds lk fa ll sk as sl da lf sa ff aj ss

DS

2 ad ad as as jak jak fad fad all all fall fall lass

DS

3 ask dad; ask dad; flak falls; flak falls; as a jak

PRACTICE MAKES PERFECT

Key each line once with a double-space between each set of three lines.

Practice e

1 d e ed ed el el led led eel eel lee lee ed el de d
2 ed ed el el led led eel eel fed fed lee lee eke ed
3 a lake; a jade; a jade sale; a desk sale; as a fee

Practice h

4 j h hj hj ha ha ah ah had had has has hj hj ha had
5 hj hj ah ah ha ha has has had had ash ash had hash
6 ah ha; has had; had ash; has half; has had a flash

Practice e and h

7 he he he she she she shed shed held held heed heed
8 a shed; a lash; he held; has jade; she held a sash
9 she has jell; he held a jade; she had a shelf sale

TECH TALK

Save the document you key for each lesson in this textbook using the word "Lesson" and the lesson number as the filename.

COMPUTER WIZ

Click the *Save* button on the toolbar to save a document using the same filename. Save your document again after keying each exercise.

SPACING TIP

Space once after ; used as punctuation.

GRAMMAR CORNER

Study the spelling and definitions of the words below. Key the Learn line, noting the word choices. Key the Apply lines, selecting the correct words.

accept *(verb) receive willingly; agree to*
except *(preposition) excluding; but*

LEARN 1   All will **accept** a trophy **except** Paul and Sue.
APPLY 2   Please (accept, except) my apologies.
APPLY 3   I can go any day (accept, except) Tuesday.

PROOFREADERS' CORNER

Study the proofreaders' marks shown at the left. Key the rough-draft paragraph below using double spacing and making corrections as you key.

stet	= Let it stand
____	= Underline
▭	= Move right

I plan to write a short book about my experience during the ③ years I was in middle school. the title will be From the Middle. I will focus on the good and bad times I had playing sports, dating, being social, keep up with the latest fashoins, and stdying. The book willinterest stud ents entering Middle or Junior high school.

WORD PROCESSING

PRINT SELECTED PAGES

When a document consists of more than one page, you can specify which page or pages you want to print.

TECH TALK

The Print dialog box can be used to specify the number of copies to be printed and whether the copies are to be collated (each copy will be printed in page order) if multiple copies are printed.

Learn to Print Selected Pages

1. Save the document before printing as a precaution.

2. Click *File* on the Menu bar. Click *Print*.

3. Click the *Pages* radio button in the Print dialog box.

4. Key the page number(s) to be printed. For example, if you want only page 1 to print, key **1** in the From box and **1** in the To box. If you want pages 4 and 5 of a 6-page document, key **4** in the From box and **5** in the To box.

5. Click *OK*.

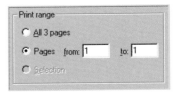

(continued on next page)

Key each line twice (slowly, then faster). Leave a DS between each pair of lines. (Do not key the vertical lines separating word groups.)

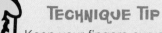

TECHNIQUE TIP

Keep your fingers curved and upright.

1 lake lake|as as|jak jak|has has|all all|fall falls
2 a lad; a lass; a jak; had all; all fall; has a jak

3 he he he|el el|led led|elf elf|self self|jell jell
4 she led; he fell; she had; a jade ad; a desk shelf

5 she she|elf elf|all all|ask ask|led led|hall halls
6 she had a flask; he had a jell sale; he asked half

7 he fell; a lad fell; she has a desk; he has a sled
8 a lake; he asked a lass; she led all fall; she had

Johann Sebastian Bach
Ludwig van Beethoven
Johannes Brahms
Frederic Chopin
Antonin Dvorak
George Frideric Handel
Franz Joseph Haydn
Felix Mendelssohn
Richard Strauss
Peter Ilyich Tchaikovsky

WRITING CORNER

A list of famous composers is shown at the left. Search the Internet (or other reference sources) to learn about one of these individuals.

Take notes in longhand, recording the information you learn about the composer. Review the notes and choose the most important information. Organize the information in a logical order in outline format. Draft a paragraph or two (in longhand) about the composer.

After writing the paragraph(s), edit the paragraph(s) to make sure your message is clear and correct. Give the completed assignment to your teacher. Your teacher will keep it and return it to you after you have finished learning the keyboard. You will then key the paragraph(s). Throughout the first 20 lessons, you will be given similar assignments about famous individuals. Eventually, you will incorporate the paragraphs into a formal report.

LESSON 39

Keyboarding Enrichment and Reports

Key each line twice SS (once slowly, then again at a faster pace). DS between 2-line groups.

1 Beth saw Joe leave quickly after my dog won six prizes.
2 Find serial numbers ending with 09, 87, 65, 43, and 21.
3 Nancy is to visit the widow when she works by the mall.

PRACTICE MAKES PERFECT

Set the Timer for 1 minute. Key at least two 1' timings on each paragraph. Then key two 2' writings on both paragraphs. Determine *gwam* and errors.

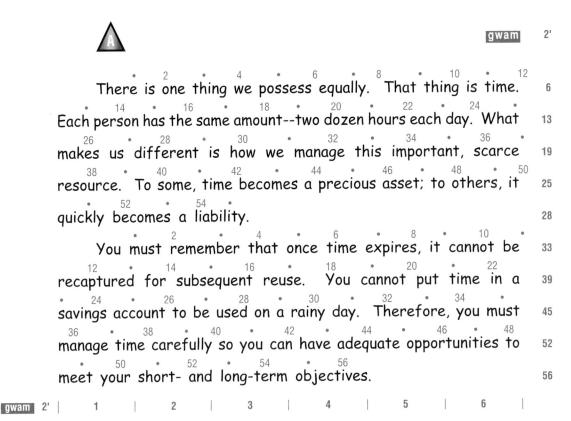

gwam 2'

A

	• 2 • 4 • 6 • 8 • 10 • 12	
	There is one thing we possess equally. That thing is time.	6

There is one thing we possess equally. That thing is time.   6
Each person has the same amount--two dozen hours each day. What   13
makes us different is how we manage this important, scarce   19
resource. To some, time becomes a precious asset; to others, it   25
quickly becomes a liability.   28

You must remember that once time expires, it cannot be   33
recaptured for subsequent reuse. You cannot put time in a   39
savings account to be used on a rainy day. Therefore, you must   45
manage time carefully so you can have adequate opportunities to   52
meet your short- and long-term objectives.   56

gwam 2' | 1 | 2 | 3 | 4 | 5 | 6 |

LESSON 4

o and r

CASEY'S WARM UP

Key each line twice single-spaced (SS): once slowly, then again at a faster pace. Double-space (DS) between 2-line groups.

Home Row

1   as as lad lad dad dad asks asks lass lass jak jak;

e and h

2   he he has has lake lake fade fade had had she she;

All Keys Learned

3   ask dad; a jade desk; he feels sad; he has a lake;

PRACTICE MAKES PERFECT

Key each line twice. DS between 2-line groups.

Practice o

1   l o l o lo lo do do so so of of old old sold sold;
2   of of sod sod hoe hoe oak oak joke joke load load;

Practice r

3   f r fr fr jar jar her her lark lark far far f r ;;
4   f r f r fr fr far far jar jar here here rake rake;

Practice o and r

5   she had a red fork; here is a road; had a red rose
6   her red roses; he rode for; red oak; her forks; or

TECH TALK

Remember to save the document for this lesson as **Lesson4**.

TECHNIQUE TIP

Keep your eyes on the textbook as you key.

TECH TALK

Remember to save your document after keying each exercise. Click the *Save* button on the toolbar to save a document using the same filename.

Title Page

Using the formatting guides given below, key a title page for the report (**L37Report**) that you completed in Lesson 37. Spell check and proofread the document. Correct all errors. Save the document as **L38Title**.

TECH TALK

Title Page: The first page of a report containing the report title, the writer's name, the date the report is prepared, and other information such as school name.

SPACING TIP

When using an 11-point or 12-point font, press *Enter/Return* six times to insert about 1" vertical space. The default top margin is 1". Press *Enter/Return* six times before keying the report title to place the title about 2" from the top of the page.

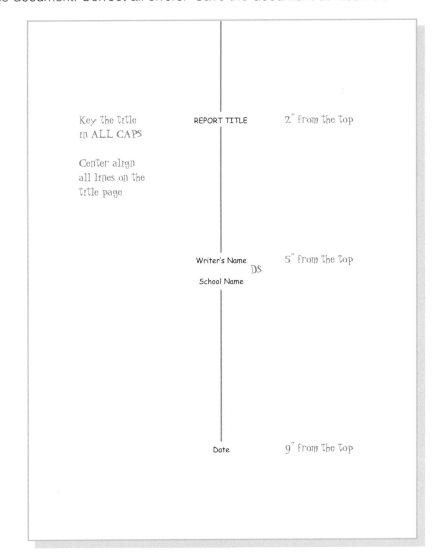

Key the title in ALL CAPS

Center align all lines on the title page

REPORT TITLE — 2" from the top

Writer's Name — 5" from the top
DS
School Name

Date — 9" from the top

WRITING CORNER

Compose a paragraph about a hobby that interests you. Describe why the hobby interests you and some of the activities involved in the hobby. Save the document as **L38Hobby**.

© PhotoDisc, Inc.

GRAMMAR CORNER

Study the definitions of the words below and the Learn lines. Note the correct way to use the words. Compose one sentence (in longhand) using the word "buy" and another sentence using the word "by."

buy *(noun/verb) something of value at a good price; to purchase; to acquire*

by *(preposition/adverb) near; close to; via; according to; at the place specified*

LEARN 1 The coat is a real **buy** at that price.
LEARN 2 Natalie will **buy** the refreshments.

LEARN 3 Please stop **by** my office before you leave.
LEARN 4 The bank is right **by** the post office.

KEYING ON YOUR OWN

Key each line twice SS (slowly, then faster). DS between 2-line groups.

Reach Review

1 olo ede hjh rfr lol ded jhj frf olo ede jhj rfr or
2 hold hold | feel feel | real real | sold sold | lake lake;

Practice e and h

3 her her | feel feel | has has | elf elf | she she | see see;
4 he had a red sled; she has jell; she held a shell;

Practice o and r

5 for for | order order | soar soar | door door | fork forks
6 for a doll; floor or door; red fork; for her dolls

All Keys Learned

7 sold a jar; half a load; ask her for; for her food
8 so he asked for forks; dad asked her for oak doors

THINKING CAP

Unscramble the letters shown at the right and key the ten words. If you have difficulty, try keying the letters in different orders to unscramble the words.

esh	kao
rfo	has
dah	ldos
lold	ofkr
oord	erso

Study the spelling and definitions of the words below. Key the Learn line, noting the word choices. Key the Apply lines, selecting the correct words.

principal (noun/adjective) *head of a school; most important*
principle (noun) *rule or code of conduct*

LEARN 1   The **principal** asked us to write behavior **principles**.
APPLY 2   The (principal, principle) will hold a meeting.
APPLY 3   The (principal, principle) reason was stated.
APPLY 4   I will follow the (principals, principles) of fair play.

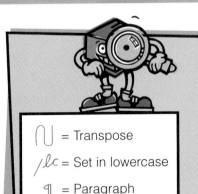

PROOFREADERS' CORNER

Study the proofreaders' marks shown at the left. Key the rough-draft paragraph below using double spacing and making corrections as you key.

∩ = Transpose
/lc = Set in lowercase
¶ = Paragraph
○sp = Spell out

May was a very good month for district 14 Sales Representatives.
They avergaed over $56,104 sales duirng May. This was an ichrease
of 7.8% increase over last May. We appreciate your work to make
thisthe best may ever.

WORD PROCESSING
SHOW AND HIDE CODES

The Typing Time *Word Processor inserts code marks in the document when certain keys are pressed. Viewing these codes can be helpful when formatting documents.*

Learn to Show and Hide Codes

To show codes:
1. Click *View* on the Menu bar. Click *Show Codes*.
2. Codes appear in the document when *Tab*, *Enter/Return*, and the *Space Bar* are pressed.

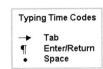

To hide codes:
Click *View* on the Menu bar. Click *Hide Codes*.

Practice What You Have Learned
1. Key the text below inserting tabs and hard returns as directed.

Tab Tab **This line is indented two tab stops from the margin.** Hard Return
This line is not indented from the left margin. Hard Return
Tab Tab Tab **This text is indented three tab stops.** Hard Return

2. Show the codes and verify that the codes appear in the document.
3. Hide the codes.

LESSON 5

Review

CASEY'S WARM UP

Key each line twice SS (once slowly, then again at a faster pace). DS between 2-line groups.

1 asdf jkl; a; sl dk fj fj dk sl a; aj sk dl f; d;s;
2 has has ask ask she she are are for for see see so
3 sole sole lake lake fear fear dear dear oar oar do

TECH TALK
Remember to save the document for this lesson as **Lesson5**.

PRACTICE MAKES PERFECT

Key each line twice. DS between 2-line groups. Keep your eyes on the textbook as you key.

TECHNIQUE TIP
When keying 3rd-row letters, reach up without moving your hands. Keep your fingers curved and upright. Key at a steady pace.

3rd-Row Emphasis

1 rf jh ed ol fr lo de rfr olo ded fr ol ed fr lo de
2 of foe for so joke load sold old ok does sole sod;

3 ear her fear here dear safe road odor sale sake of
4 rose jerk hose lakes radar joke doors horse saddle

All Keystrokes Learned

5 or of lad doe had sad her oar fad jak sod foe for;
6 off sale joke does real roads desk flak half hero;

7 joke ashes adds free lose lash roses; read; lakes;
8 jokes dead free loads sofas soaker loaded address;

Keyboarding Enrichment and Reports

CASEY'S WARM UP

Key each line twice SS (once slowly, then again at a faster pace). DS between 2-line groups.

1 Joy will pack a dozen big boxes of her heavy equipment.
2 Key 12, 34, 56, 78, and 90 as fast as you can each day.
3 Pamela kept the shamrocks in the fir box on the mantle.

PRACTICE MAKES PERFECT

Set the Timer for 1 minute. Key at least two 1' timings on each paragraph. Then key two 2' writings on both paragraphs. Determine *gwam* and errors.

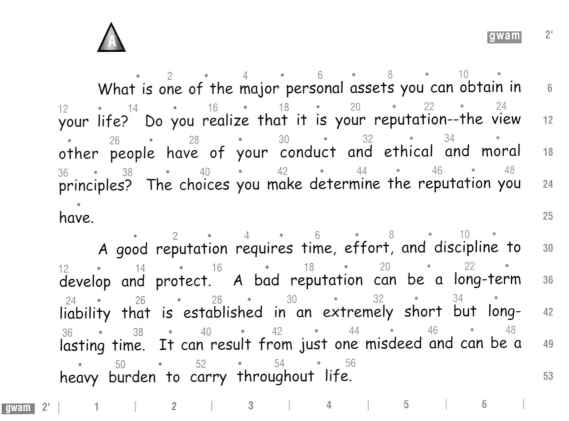

gwam 2'

What is one of the major personal assets you can obtain in 6
your life? Do you realize that it is your reputation--the view 12
other people have of your conduct and ethical and moral 18
principles? The choices you make determine the reputation you 24
have. 25

A good reputation requires time, effort, and discipline to 30
develop and protect. A bad reputation can be a long-term 36
liability that is established in an extremely short but long- 42
lasting time. It can result from just one misdeed and can be a 49
heavy burden to carry throughout life. 53

gwam 2' | 1 | 2 | 3 | 4 | 5 | 6 |

GRAMMAR CORNER

Read the capitalization rules below. Study the Learn sentences and note how the rules are applied. Compose one sentence (in longhand) for each rule, applying the rule.

Capitalize days of the week.

LEARN 1   Tom will be absent until Friday.

LEARN 2   Sue Chen arrived on Thursday.

Capitalize months of the year.

LEARN 3   School begins in August.

LEARN 4   My next appointment is in May.

Capitalize cities, states, and countries.

LEARN 5   Mr. Barns left for Milwaukee, Wisconsin, on Saturday.

LEARN 6   The tour includes Austria, Germany, and Switzerland.

KEYING ON YOUR OWN

Key each line twice (slowly, then faster). DS between 2-line groups. Goal: To speed up spacing between words.

1   as a | as a | do so | do so | or so | or so | as he | as he | do a

2   had a | had a | jar of | jar of | a look | a look | all of | all

3   has a | has a | a sad | a sad | are here | are here | do as he

WORD PROCESSING

PRINT COMMAND

Use the Print command to print an open document.

COMPUTER WIZ

Click the *Print* button on the toolbar to access the Print dialog box quickly.

Print a Document

1. Click *File* on the Menu bar. Click *Print*. The Print dialog box appears.

2. Click the down arrow for the Printer Name drop-down list to choose a printer if your printer is not displayed. Click *OK*.

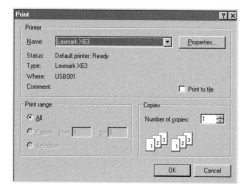

Practice What You Have Learned

1. Print **Lesson5**.

2. Print **Lesson4**.

2" TM

Title   FORMATTING SHORT REPORTS
                                                         QS

Report   Short reports are often prepared without covers or binders. If they consist of
body
        more than one page, the pages are usually fastened together in the upper-left corner

        by a staple or paper clip. Such reports are called unbound reports.
                                                                          DS
Side   Margins
                DS
heading   The left and right margins of unbound reports are 1 inch. The bottom margin is

        at *least* 1 inch. The top margin of the first page is 2 inches and 1 inch is used for all

        other pages.
                    DS
Side   Internal Spacing
                        DS
heading   A quadruple-space (QS) is left between the report title and the first line of

        the body. Multiple-line titles are double-spaced (DS).

(1" LM)   A DS is left above and below side headings and between paragraphs.   (1" RM)

        Paragraphs may be single-spaced (SS) or DS. This report is DS.
                                                                      DS
Side   Side Headings
                    DS
heading   Side headings should be aligned at the left margin and should be underlined *or*

        keyed in bold style. Whichever style is chosen, use it consistently throughout the

        report.
               DS
Side   Page Numbers
                    DS
heading   The first page of a report may or may not include a page number. The reports

        you key in this and the following lessons will not have the first page numbered. On

        the second and subsequent pages, the page number is to be right aligned in the

        header at the top of the page.

                                At least 1"

LESSON 6

i and t

CASEY'S WARM UP

Key each line twice SS (once slowly, then again at a faster pace). DS between 2-line groups.

1 of had she oak for has ask jak rod lead self here;
2 as of | had a | do so | he ask | a jar | he or she | here are;
3 she had a jar; he ask for; he sold a desk; so far;

PRACTICE MAKES PERFECT

Key each line twice. DS between 2-line groups. Keep your eyes on the textbook as you key.

TECH TALK
Follow your teacher's instructions regarding when to print completed lessons.

Practice i
1 k i ik ik is is if if did did fire fire like like;
2 ik ik ki ki kid kid side side hide hide fire fire;
3 if he did; so did she; a kid is; like his; a jail;

Practice t
4 f t tf tf to to at at the the dot dot tooth tooth;
5 t f tf tf she she feet feet sheet sheet tear tear;
6 to do the; her teeth; to take it to the; the tree;

Practice i and t
7 i t i t it it tie tie hit hit kite kite tide tide;
8 it is; is it his tile; his kite is; it is his toad
9 if it fits; is it his; to the jet; his jet is fast

Practice What You Have Learned

1. Open a new document. Key the three lines of text below. Press *Enter/Return* at the end of each line.

   A page number usually does not appear on page 1 of a report.
   A page number does appear on page 2 of a report.
   A page number does appear on page 3 of a report.

2. Insert a hard page break at the end of the first line and another at the end of the second line.

3. Create Header A and choose *First Page Only* for the placement. Leave the header empty and click *Record.*

4. Create Header B and choose *All Pages* for the placement. Choose right alignment, insert the page number, and click *Record.*

5. Scroll through the pages to verify that a page number appears on pages 2 and 3 but not on page 1.

6. Save the document as **L37Header2**.

WORD PROCESSING

APPLY WHAT YOU HAVE LEARNED

Short Report

Study the formatting guides in the report on the next page. Key the report following the formatting guides. Spell check the report and proofread carefully. Correct all errors. Save the report as **L37Report**.

Key each line twice (slowly, then faster). Leave a DS between each pair of lines.

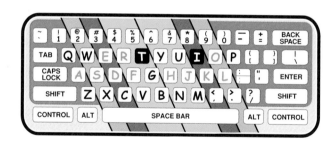

3rd-Row Emphasis

1 de ki fr lo ft so to is eat his fit toss here tree

2 or is are there roots roast tear tire resort torts

3 it is hot; he is last; their toast; see their jet;

All Keystrokes Learned

4 if he is; see her jet; see the lark; looked at her

5 he said she is; if he jets to the lake; three dots

6 shall ask her for a raise; to order a jet for her;

Space Bar Emphasis

7 to hi it id so at if ha do he of as or ha ho is er

8 to do so|she is to|to do it|if it is|she is to see

9 she is to do it for free; the jet took to the air;

WRITING CORNER

Hank Aaron
Roberto Clemente
Joe DiMaggio
Greg Maddux
Willie Mays
Mark McGwire
Cal Ripken, Jr.
Jackie Robinson
Babe Ruth
Nolan Ryan

A list of famous baseball players is shown at the left. Search the Internet (or other reference sources) to learn about one of these players.

Take notes in longhand, recording the information you learn about the baseball player from the Internet or other reference material. Review the notes and choose the most important information about the individual. Organize the information in a logical order in outline format.

Draft a paragraph or two (in longhand) about the baseball player. Edit the paragraph(s) to make sure your message is clear and correct. Give the completed assignment to your teacher.

2. Insert a hard page break at the end of the first line and another at the end of the second line.

3. Create a header containing a right-aligned page number. Scroll through the pages to verify that the page numbers appear correctly.

4. Save the document as **L37Header1**.

Learn to Create Multiple Headers

To prevent a header with a page number from appearing on the first page of a document, such as a report, record an "empty" header without a page number or text for page 1. Then record another header with the page number to appear on all other pages.

To record Header A:

1. Click *Format* on the Menu bar. Click *Headers* and then *Header A*.

2. Click *Placement* on the Menu bar and choose *First Page Only*.

3. Click *Record*.

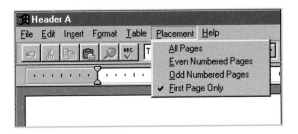

To record Header B:

1. Click *Format* on the Menu bar. Click *Headers* and then *Header B*.

2. Click *Placement* on the Menu bar and choose *All Pages*.

3. Choose right alignment and insert the page number.

4. Click *Record*.

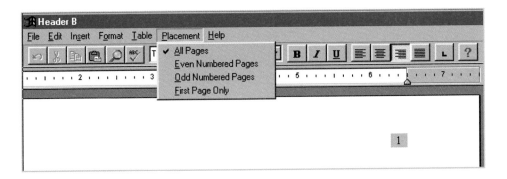

(continued on next page)

TECH TALK

In a header with First Page Only placement, the header text (or a blank header) will appear on page 1 of the document, disregarding text or page numbers recorded in other headers.

LESSON 7

Left Shift and period (.)

CASEY'S WARM UP

Key each line twice SS (once slowly, then again at a faster pace). DS between 2-line groups.

1 hj ft ki fr lo de jh ki fr lo de jh tf ik rf ol de
2 does area fort jerk lake said take fast joke still
3 if he sells the oak door; he has a jet at the lake

PRACTICE MAKES PERFECT

Key each line twice. DS between 2-line groups. Keep your eyes on the textbook as you key.

Practice Left Shift Key

1 Jd Jd Ha Ha Kf Kf Le Le Or Or Is Is Jett Jett Otto
2 Jake sold; Kate said; Kit hit; Lee read; Oak Lake;
3 Did he see Hal at the Oak Lake Hotel; I told Jake;

Practice . (period)

4 l . .l. .l. .sd. .sd. fl. fl. dif. dif. ft. ft. .;
5 .a. .j. .s. .d. .k. .f. .j. .e. .r. .t. .i. .o. .;
6 hr. hr. fl. fl. ed. ed. rd. rd. fed. fed. ft. ft.;

Practice Left Shift and .

7 Ill. or Okl. or Ore. or Ill. ;a; Okl. .;. Ore. .d.
8 I did. Kate sold. Hal fell. Jake left. I said.
9 Illa read the letter. Jae ate the steak. I hide.

TECHNIQUE TIP

When keying capital letters, hold down the *Shift* key, strike the letter key, and release quickly.

SPACING TIP

Space once after . used with abbreviations and initials. Space twice after . at the end of a sentence except at line endings. There, return without spacing.

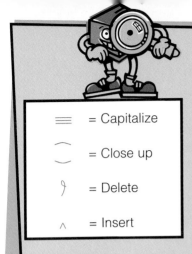

PROOFREADERS' CORNER

Study the proofreaders' marks shown at the left. Key the rough-draft paragraph below using double spacing and making corrections as you key.

≡	= Capitalize
⌢	= Close up
⸙	= Delete
∧	= Insert

just how well do you adjust to big change? recog nize that change is certain to come as deth or taxes. You can avoid change, but your can ad just to it. how quickly your do this is index of likely success in the world a head.

WORD PROCESSING

PAGE NUMBER IN HEADER

Headers contain information that appears at the top of pages in a document. A header is used in reports to display page numbers.

COMPUTER WIZ

Insert page number and date information into a header quickly by clicking the appropriate button.

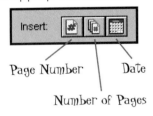

Learn to Create a Header with Page Numbers

1. Click *Format* on the Menu bar. Click *Headers* and then *Header A*. The Header A window opens.

2. Click an alignment button on the toolbar to choose the position (left, center, or right) for the page number. (For reports, click the *Align Right* button.)

3. Click the *Page Number* button in the lower-right corner of the window to insert the page number.

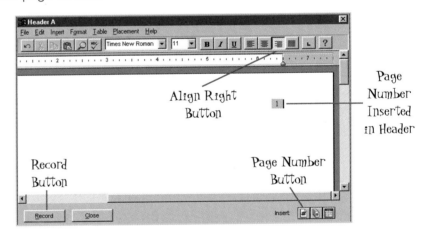

4. Click the *Record* button in the lower-left corner of the window to record (save) the header. The page number now appears in the document.

Practice What You Have Learned

1. Key the three lines of text below. Press *Enter/Return* at the end of each line.

   This text is the first line on page 1.
   This text is the first line on page 2.
   This text is the first line on page 3.

(continued on next page)

WORD PROCESSING
INSERTION POINT

The insertion point (the blinking vertical bar) shows where the text you key will appear. You can use keys or key combinations to move the insertion point quickly.

You can also use the mouse to move the insertion point. Click on the location where you want to place the insertion point.

TECHNIQUE TIP
Space quickly between words and phrases. Strike the keys at a brisk, steady pace.

WORD PROCESSING
APPLY WHAT YOU HAVE LEARNED

Use the text lines you keyed in Keying on Your Own. For each line, move the insertion point to the location shown by the red arrow on the following copy and key the word indicated. Be sure to move the insertion point quickly. Refer to the chart above as needed.

Move the Insertion Point

Using the text you keyed for Practice Makes Perfect, practice moving the insertion point with the keys shown below.

To Move:	Keys
One letter to the right	→
One letter to the left	←
One line up	↑
One line down	↓
One word to the right	Ctrl + →
One word to the left	Ctrl + ←
To the end of the line	End
To the beginning of the line	Home

KEYING ON YOUR OWN

Key each line twice (slowly, then faster). Leave a DS between each pair of lines.

3rd-Row Emphasis

1 Jett shall ask Jo for her three old hats for Jess.
2 Ida said she is to take the old road to Lake Otto.

Key Phrases

3 is to | do it | if it is | to do | he or she | to hear | it is
4 for it | ask for a | for the | to the | is the | this is for

All Keys Learned

5 L. J. took Illa to the lake to fish; I took Jared.
6 Krista Lee had a salad to eat; Josh had real fish.

Line 1: Key **Lake**.
Line 2: Key **Lee**.
Line 5: Key **to eat a salad**.
Line 6: Key **fresh**. Key **Frost**.

1 Jett shall ask Jo▲ for her three old hats for Jess.
2 Ida ▲ said she is to take the old road to Lake Otto.
5 L. J. took Illa to the lake to fish; I took Jared▲.
6 Krista Lee had a ▲ salad to eat; Josh ▲ had real fish.

Keyboarding Enrichment and Reports

CASEY'S WARM UP

Key each line twice SS (once slowly, then again at a faster pace). DS between 2-line groups.

1 Peter was amazed just how quickly he fixed the big van.
2 I used 50 plates, 78 knives, 194 forks, and 362 spoons.
3 The visit may end a problem and make the firm a profit.

ENDURANCE GOAL

When you can key 15–20 *wam* above your 1' *gwam* rate for 15", increase the timings to 30". Move to the next line when you are able to complete at least 2 lines within the 30".

CONTROL GOAL

When you can key at 15–20 *wam* above your 1' *gwam* rate for 30", drop back two lines. Try to key that line with not more than one error for 30". Move to the next line when your control goal is met.

PRACTICE MAKES PERFECT

Set the Timer for 15 seconds. Key at least ten 15" timings, beginning on a line that is approximately 1/4 of your 1' *gwam* rate. Move to the next line when you are able to complete a line within 15". Force your stroking speed to a higher level on each timing.

1 Dorlana may go with them.
2 I did visit the downtown firm.
3 They will visit six sorority girls.
4 When I go the city, I may visit the spa.
5 The six girls may visit them by the big rock.
6 If they go to the social with us, they will visit.

| 15" | 4 | 8 | 12 | 16 | 20 | 24 | 28 | 32 | 36 | 40 | |

GRAMMAR CORNER

Study the spelling and definitions of the words below. Key the Learn lines, noting the word choices. Key the Apply lines, selecting the correct words.

loan (noun) money borrowed; something lent
lone (adjective) alone or isolated; only

LEARN 1 Sam made the **loan** on Tuesday.
LEARN 2 The **lone** tiger roamed the cage.
APPLY 3 I was the (loan, lone) person making a (loan, lone).
APPLY 4 I must repay the (loan, lone) within three years.

Study the definitions of the words below and the Learn lines. Note the correct way to use the words. Compose one sentence (in longhand) using the word "hear" and another sentence using the word "here."

hear	*(verb) to gain knowledge of by the ear*
here	*(adverb) in or at this place; at this point; in this case; on this point*

LEARN 1	Did you **hear** what I said?
LEARN 2	You will **hear** the same thing again on Friday.
LEARN 3	Let's plan to meet **here** on Monday.
LEARN 4	The names of the winners are **here** on this list.

THINKING CAP

Unscramble the letters shown at the right to create ten words. If you have difficulty, key the letters in different orders to unscramble the words.

kas	okto
eht	hfsi
fro	dsia
elsa	olas
lfla	dlsaa

To delete a hard page break:

1. Place the insertion point at the beginning of the page after the hard page break.

2. Press the *Backspace* key.

Practice What You Have Learned

1. Key the three lines below, inserting a hard page break at the end of each line.

   This text is the first line on page 1.
   This text is the first line on page 2.
   This text is the first line on page 3.

2. The page indicator should read Page 4 of 4. Revise the text on page 3 to read:

   This text is also on page 2.

3. Delete the second hard page break. (Place the insertion point at the beginning of page 3 and press the *Backspace* key.)

4. Confirm that the last two lines of text appear together on the second page.

Refer to the page indicator at the lower-left corner of the screen to see the page the insertion point is on and the total pages in the document.

Page 3 of 4

LESSON 8

u and c

CASEY'S WARM UP

Key each line twice SS (once slowly, then again at a faster pace). DS between 2-line groups.

1 fr de tf ki lo rf ed ft ik ol ft. Ill. jh er io tr
2 as do for her joke lake; tear lost see deer faster
3 Jade took the first shot; Lester took three shots.

PRACTICE MAKES PERFECT

Key each line twice. DS between 2-line groups. Keep your eyes on the textbook as you key.

Practice u
1 ju ju uju uju use use fur fur just just dust dusts
2 rut rut rust rust fuse fuse user user trust trusts
3 is just; full surf; flue shot; is rusted; is sure;

Practice c
4 dc dc cdc cdc ice ice; ace ace code code race race
5 dock dock coat coat rock rock face face cost costs
6 the code; to cite; dress code; to cease; to crest;

Practice u and c
7 cu cu cuts cuts ducks ducks cute cute cluck clucks
8 is cured; a curse; our dock; for luck; cute ducks;
9 Jock lost his clock. Jack had such dreadful luck.

Key each line once. DS between each set of lines.

Practice > (greater than sign)

1 | > | > |> |> |>| |>| >|> >|> >15 >20 >25 >30 >35 >400

2 Is 1/2>1/4? Is 1/8>3/8? Is .0001>5%? Is .3333>333%?

Practice < (less than sign)

3 k < k < k< k< k<k k<k <k< <k< <15 <20 <25 <30 <35 <400

4 Is 1/2<3/4? Is 1/8<3/8? Is .0001<.05%? Is 2.5<250%?

Practice > and <

5 Mary knows if 5<10, then 10>5 and if .1>1%, then 1%<.1.

6 When a>b, b>c, c>d, and d>e, Vince says e is <u>always</u> <a.

WORD PROCESSING

HARD PAGE BREAK

Typing Time has two types of page breaks (soft and hard) to signal the end of a page. **Soft page breaks** *are inserted automatically when the current page is full.* **Hard page breaks** *are inserted manually when you want to end a page before it is full.*

TECH TALK

A soft page break moves automatically when additional text is keyed before the soft page break.

Learn to Use Hard Page Breaks

To insert a hard page break:

1. Place the insertion point where you want the page to end and a new page to begin.

2. Click *Insert* on the Menu bar. Click *Break*. The Break dialog box appears.

3. Click the *Page break* radio button if it is not already selected. Click *OK*.

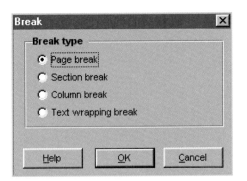

(continued on next page)

GRAMMAR CORNER

Read the capitalization rules below. Study the Learn sentences and note how the rules are applied. Compose one sentence (in longhand) for each rule, applying the rule.

Capitalize the names of holidays.

LEARN 1   I will be out of town on the Fourth of July.

LEARN 2   The next official holiday is Thanksgiving.

Capitalize historic periods and events.

LEARN 3   Pearl Harbor preceded our entry into World War II.

LEARN 4   The Revolutionary War shaped our history.

Capitalize streets, roads, and avenues.

LEARN 5   Maria lives on Pennsylvania Street.

LEARN 6   They will work on Hastings Avenue this summer.

KEYING ON YOUR OWN

Key each line twice (slowly, then faster). Leave a DS between each pair of lines.

3rd/1st Rows

1 ice coat teach reach occur clock cause licks stick

2 for the; the causes of it; off the docks; just her

Key Words

3 sad juice clear took fort hook sold fast lake here

4 use rich due jackal dust code usual facial haircut

Key Phrases

5 it is due | call us | use the | use of the | off the | is it

6 sure is | just like | all of | ask her for | for it | at the

All Keys Learned

7 Jake told Joe that he had lost four of the checks.

8 Karl said it is a just cause; Laura is sure of it.

LESSON 36

Keyboarding Enrichment and Review > and <

CASEY'S WARM UP

Key each line twice SS (once slowly, then again at a faster pace). DS between 2-line groups.

1 Jacque Steven fixed the clocks that may win big prizes.
2 Our best scores were 97 to 86, 75 to 64, and 102 to 93.
3 The busy maid is to rush to the six girls in the dorms.

PRACTICE MAKES PERFECT

Key each line twice SS (once slowly, then again at a faster pace). DS between 2-line groups.

Left-Hand Words

1 ace bad car dad eat far gas raw sat tea vat wet zag wee
2 adds bare cart deed edge face gage raze save text trace
3 verb wage zest arts base cave debt east free grab races

Right-Hand Words

4 hi in my no oh pi up you him ill joy kin mink pump upon
5 him ill lip mom pun you hull jump kiln link mummy nylon
6 hill join lump mill noun only uphill holly nippy poplin

TECHNIQUE TIP

Key at a continuous pace without pausing. Keep your elbows in a relaxed natural position at the sides of your body.

GRAMMAR CORNER

Study the spelling and definitions of the words below. Key the Learn line, noting the word choices. Key the Apply lines, selecting the correct words.

new	(adjective) not old or familiar
knew	(verb) understood

LEARN 1 Tim **knew** he wanted to buy the **new** video.
APPLY 2 If I (knew, new), I would get the (knew, new) one.
APPLY 3 He (knew, new) it was a (knew, new) idea.

LESSON 9

Review

CASEY'S WARM UP

Key each line twice SS (once slowly, then again at a faster pace). DS between 2-line groups.

1 i ed tf uj fr ol ik hj cd l. de ft ju rf lo ki jh;
2 sales ducks fort has just luck here silk hot juice
3 Joe said that he could take the oats to the store.

PRACTICE MAKES PERFECT

Key each pair of lines twice (slowly, then faster). DS between 2-line groups. Keep your eyes on the textbook as you strike the *Enter/Return* key.

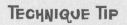

TECHNIQUE TIP

Keep up your pace to the end of the line. Strike the *Enter/Return* key immediately and start the new line without pausing.

1 Jackie left for the lake.
2 I had a ski race set for four.

3 Jared left a file at the desk.
4 Karl could use the three old coats.

5 Jo asked her to talk to each of us.
6 Jess could see the lake off to the east.

7 Ida said that she has a hut at the lake.
8 Les has a dock for the use of all the skiers.

9 Laura said that she could see all the clocks.
10 Hal said to take the three old coats for the sale.

Key the copy below following these directions.

1. Set 1.5" side margins.

2. Set a right tab at 5.4".

3. Use paragraph alignments as shown.

4. Use 2.5" side margins for the paragraph following the time and date.

5. Set a decimal tab to align decimals in the ticket prices.

6. Use bold and italic for the policy statement.

7. Apply additional formatting of your choice, such as font, style, size, and line spacing, to create an attractive 8.5" x 11" poster.

8. Use Spell Check and proofread. Save the document as **L35Poster**.

O'Rourke Benefit Dance   Kittanning Junior High School

KJHS Gymnasium   Fayette, PA

7:30 to 10:30 p.m.

Friday, May 25, 200-

The proceeds from this dance will help Kenny O'Rourke's family pay medical costs related to Kenny's injuries that resulted from an automobile accident on April 26. Kenny, an 8th grade student at KJHS, suffered injuries to the spine and a severe concussion in the accident. He has been hospitalized since the accident.

Music by DJ Tom Jerrico   Sponsored by KJHS Service Club

Tickets: $3.25 per person if purchased in advance
            $5.50 per person if purchased at the door

School Board Policy requires that all students remain at the dance until 10:30 p.m. unless they leave with a parent.

Poster approved by _____

May ____, _____.

Key each line twice (slowly, then faster). Leave a DS between each pair of lines.

TECHNIQUE TIP

Think and say the words or phrases as you key them. Strike the keys at a brisk, steady pace.

Key Words

1 as do if so has did cut for had her lake just rust
2 fit sad hit lad sit lick fear look jeer cute ducks
3 did are sack lost take load tire road juice defeat

Key Phrases

4 to use | it is too | do so | to do | if she | is it | it could
5 he did it | he or she | of the | to all | is a hit | to load
6 if she did it | to ask her | here it is | to the | too sad

Easy Sentences

7 Kellee told us that Jackie has the four red forks.
8 Karl just took the skier there to see the old jet.
9 Hal said he left her old fur coat at the ski lake.

Giovanni Bellini
Paul Cezanne
Leonardo da Vinci
Edouard Manet
Claude Monet
Michelangelo
Pablo Picasso
Raphael
Jacopo Tintoretto
Vincent van Gogh

WRITING CORNER

A list of famous artists is shown at the left. Search the Internet (or other reference sources) to learn about one of these artists.

Take notes in longhand, recording the information you learn about the artist from the Internet or other reference material. Review the notes and choose the most important information about the individual. Organize the information in a logical order in outline format.

Draft a paragraph or two (in longhand) about the artist. Edit the paragraph(s) to make sure your message is clear and correct. Give the completed assignment to your teacher.

GRAMMAR CORNER

Study the spelling and definitions of the words below. Key the Learn line, noting the word choices. Key the Apply lines, selecting the correct words.

wait   *(verb) remain in readiness or expectation*
weight   *(noun) amount that something weighs*

LEARN 1   I will not **wait** for his **weight** to be posted.
APPLY 2   I will (wait, weight) a day to lose (wait, weight).
APPLY 3   The truck's (wait, weight) exceeded the load limit.

KEYING ON YOUR OWN: REVIEW =, [, AND]

Key each line once. DS between each set of lines.

Practice = (equals sign)

1 ; = ; = ;= ;= ;=; ;=; =;= I use the = in all equations.

2 Use this formula in the worksheet: =(A9+B21+C31)/(D4).

Practice [and] (left and right brackets)

3 ; [; [;[;[;[; ;[; [;[[;[The little finger keys [.

4 ;] ;] ;] ;] ;]; ;];];]];] The little finger keys].

Practice =, [, and]

5 Here's the part of the equation that he knows [5(a+b)].

6 Brackets [ ] are used in quotations to reveal revisions.

7 If x=14, y=36, and x+y+z=125, will you tell me what z=?

*Use the **Backspace** key to delete (remove) text to the left of the insertion point. Use the **Delete** key to remove (delete) text to the right of the insertion point.*

Make Corrections Using Backspace and Delete

Use the text you keyed for Lesson 9, Practice Makes Perfect. For each line, move the insertion point to the location shown by the red arrow on the copy below and make the change indicated:

Line   1: Change **Jackie** to **Jack** using the **Backspace** key.

Line   2: Change **I** to **Lori** using the **Delete** key.

Line   3: Change **a file** to **four files** and insert **old** before **desk**.

Line   4: Delete **three** and change **coats** to **coat**.

Line   5: Change **Jo** to **Joe**.

Line   6: Change **east** to **south**.

Line   7: Delete **that**.

Line   8: Delete **the use of**; insert **to use** after **skiers**.

Line   9: Change **Laura** to **Lori**.

Line 10: Delete **old**.

1 Jackie▲ left for the lake.

2 ▲ I had a ski race set for four.

3 Jared left ▲ a file at the ▲ desk.

4 Karl could use the three▲ old ▲ coats.

5 Jo▲ asked her to talk to each of us.

6 Jess could see the lake off to the ▲ east.

7 Ida said that▲ she has a hut at the lake.

8 Les has a dock for ▲ the use of all the skiers▲.

9 Laura▲ said that she could see all the clocks.

10 Hal said to take the three ▲ old coats for the sale.

THINKING CAP

Using only the letters shown at the right, key as many words as you can in five minutes. Do not key words that require capital letters.

a   s   d   f   j   k   l   ;   h   e   o   r   i   t   u   c

LESSON 35

Keyboarding Enrichment and Review =, [, and]

CASEY'S WARM UP

Key each line twice SS (once slowly, then again at a faster pace). DS between 2-line groups.

1 Vidhay will buy six unique jackets from Gus for prizes.
2 Call 375-4698 by May 2 to schedule the 10 a.m. meeting.
3 If a big tug slams the dock, it may make a big problem.

PRACTICE MAKES PERFECT

Set the Timer for 1 minute. Key at least two 1' timings on each paragraph. Then key two 2' writings on both paragraphs. Determine *gwam* and errors.

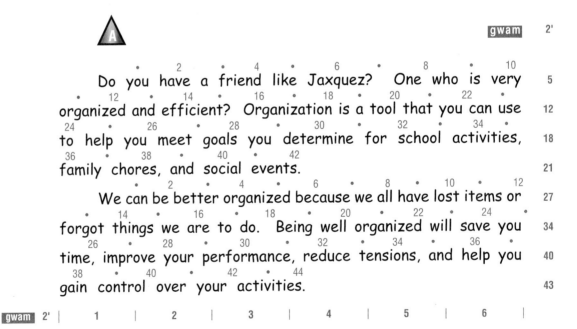

| | gwam | 2' |

```
          •    2    •    4    •    6    •    8    •    10
     Do you have a friend like Jaxquez?  One who is very        5
    •    12   •    14   •    16   •    18   •    20   •    22   •
organized and efficient?  Organization is a tool that you can use   12
    24   •    26   •    28   •    30   •    32   •    34   •
to help you meet goals you determine for school activities,    18
    36   •    38   •    40   •    42
family chores, and social events.                              21
          •    2    •    4    •    6    •    8    •    10   •    12
     We can be better organized because we all have lost items or   27
    •    14   •    16   •    18   •    20   •    22   •    24   •
forgot things we are to do.  Being well organized will save you   34
    26   •    28   •    30   •    32   •    34   •    36   •
time, improve your performance, reduce tensions, and help you   40
    38   •    40   •    42   •    44
gain control over your activities.                             43
```

gwam 2' | 1 | 2 | 3 | 4 | 5 | 6 |

LESSON 10

n and w

CASEY'S WARM UP

Key each line twice SS (once slowly, then again at a faster pace). DS between 2-line groups.

1 jh de ki uj cd ju lo ft rf as hj ed ik ju dc tc ol
2 she is; a car; if Jack; lost it; just did; red hat
3 Jack told Kirk to rush to his car fast for a coat.

PRACTICE MAKES PERFECT

Key each line twice. DS between 2-line groups. Keep your eyes on the textbook as you key.

Practice n

1 j n jn jn an an ant ant and and ten ten sand sands
2 nj nj nj and and end end send send nine nine no no
3 she is in; an oak; an ant; an end; and so; the end

Practice w

4 s w ws ws sw sw ow ow wow wow sow sow cow cow owes
5 w ws ws ow ow low low owe owe how how sow sow sows
6 it was; we were; a two; is how; too low; will wade

Practice n and w

7 own own win win won won now now when when new news
8 to win; to own; is low; of now; she won; to own it
9 Janet saw a show in the town; she won two tickets.

4. When a word appears in the Word box, do one of the following actions to continue:
   - If the correct spelling appears in the Suggestions list, click the correct word to select it and then click the *Replace* button (or the *Replace All* button to correct all occurrences of the misspelled word) and Spell Check will correct the text.
   - If the correct spelling does not appear in the Suggestions list but the spelling in the Word box is incorrect, key the correct spelling in the Word box and then click either the *Replace* or *Replace All* button, whichever is appropriate.
   - If the spelling in the Word edit field is correct, click *Skip Once* (or *Skip Always* to skip all occurrences of the word) and Spell Check will not change the text.

5. Click *Done* if you want to stop Spell Check before it checks the entire document. Otherwise, click *OK* when Spell Check finishes checking the entire document and then click *Done*.

TECH TALK

Spell Check will not find words that are spelled correctly but used incorrectly. Also, the *Typing Time* dictionary does not contain numbers or many proper nouns or scientific terms. Therefore, you should proofread carefully after using Spell Check.

Practice What You Have Learned

1. Key the paragraph below exactly as shown—*do not* correct any errors.

   Principle Kinoma met with won of the socker co-captains this past weak too discuss the program for Parents Night. They decided that the palyers is to be introduced with there parents or guardian before the start of the macth. Each player will walk with his/her parents to the center of the field too receive for carnations.

2. Save the text as **L34**.

3. Use Spell Check to check the text. Make a handwritten list of the words Spell Check found that were misspelled.

4. When Spell Check is finished, carefully proofread the text and make a handwritten list of the errors that you found that Spell Check did not. Make these corrections to the document.

5. Save the document as **L34Correct**.

WRITING CORNER

Identify the occupation you wish to pursue and the school subjects that you believe are important for success in that occupation. Compose a paragraph or two explaining why the subjects are important. Save the document as **L34Occupation**.

© PhotoDisc, Inc.

GRAMMAR CORNER

Study the definitions of the words below and the Learn lines. Note the correct way to use the words. Compose one sentence (in longhand) using the word "our" and another sentence using the word "hour."

our   *(adjective) of or relating to ourselves as possessors*

hour   *(noun) the 24th part of a day; a particular time*

LEARN 1   It was **our** team that won the game.

LEARN 2   You can pick it up at **our** house.

LEARN 3   We need one more **hour** to finish the game.

LEARN 4   The bus will leave in one **hour**.

KEYING ON YOUR OWN

Key each line twice SS (slowly, then faster). DS between 2-line groups.

Technique Tip

When keying capital letters, hold down the *Shift* key, strike the letter key, and release quickly.

Shift Key Emphasis

1   Kate or Jan; Oct. or Jan.; Nate and Nan were here.

2   Linda and Jack; Ursula or Nick; Kent and Jennifer

3   Kate J. Jacks will work in Hawaii for Jed L. Lane.

Key Words

4   and the his her are cut own she car feet lake jail

5   ten can two run four new one old nine fun three as

6   cloth hand rush sand join could hits such cue owls

All Letters Learned

7   Janet had won just one set of three when luck hit.

8   Ken can do the work if he will just use his skill.

9   Jake could see four oil wells on the federal land.

THINKING CAP

Unscramble the letters at the right to create ten words.

kowr	etrhe
adln	eerhw
jtsu	uodfn
crea	eonwd
ewnh	tchlo

KEYING ON YOUR OWN: REVIEW ! AND \

Key each line once. DS between each set of lines.

Practice ! (exclamation point)

1 a ! a ! a! a! a!a a!a !a! Please!   You're the greatest!
2 Oh, what a test!   Yes, I'm fine!   Ready!   Begin keying!

Practice \ (backslash)

3 ; \ ; \ ;\ ;\ ;\; ;\; \;\ The \ is used with computers.
4 I will save the document at c:\school\math\problems_25.

**Practice ! and **

5 Generally, they can use an ! in a filename but not a \.
6 Please, use this path to find the file c:\lit\5th\hmwk!

WORD PROCESSING
SPELL CHECK

Use Spell Check to check text for misspelled words. Spell Check compares the keyed words to words in Typing Time's dictionary. If a word in the text does not match a word in the dictionary, the word is displayed in the dialog box and suggestions (what the software suggests as the correct word) and options (Skip Once, Skip Always, Replace, etc.) are given.

Click the *Spell Check* button on the toolbar to start Spell Check quickly.

Learn to Spell Check

1. Save the document as a precaution.
2. Click *Edit* on the Menu bar. Click *Spell Check*.
3. When the Spell Check dialog box appears, click *Start*. Spell Check starts at the beginning of the document. As soon as Spell Check identifies a word not found in its dictionary, that word appears in the Word box and suggestions may appear in the Suggestions list.

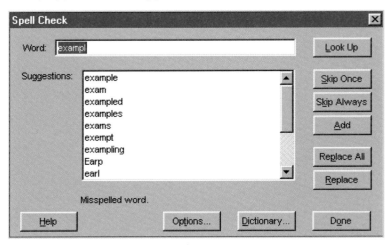

(continued on next page)

LESSON 11

g and Right Shift

CASEY'S WARM UP

Key each line twice SS (once slowly, then again at a faster pace). DS between 2-line groups.

1   cd uj ed ik tf ol rf hj ws nj; Janet saw the cart.
2   as if | he can | down at the lake | Kate saw Jed | we were
3   Jack took last week off to attend the horse races.

PRACTICE MAKES PERFECT

Key each line twice. DS between 2-line groups. Keep your eyes on the textbook as you key.

Practice g

1   f g g gf gf go go dog dog fog fog got got jog jogs
2   g g gf gf go go got got jog jog gone gone log logs
3   get it; go get; to jog; to golf; the green goggles

Practice Right Shift

4   F; F; Al Al; Dale Dale; Earl or Dick; Chi and Ann.
5   Scott saw Raul; Erin called Rafael; I called Chow.
6   Donna told Anna; Anna told Frank; Frank told Stan.

Practice g and Right Shift

7   Gregg has gone to Russia on a gold hunt with Gene.
8   Garth got an A for his grade; Dan got a C for his.
9   George is to sign for Reggie; I can sign for Raul.

LESSON 34

Keyboarding Enrichment and Review ! and \

CASEY'S WARM UP

Key each line twice SS (once slowly, then again at a faster pace). DS between 2-line groups.

1   Di will quickly bake six big pizzas for the jovial men.
2   My school ordered 7 chairs: 2 JC-18590 and 5 VR-90346.
3   The busy maid bid for the soap dish and big ivory bowl.

ENDURANCE GOAL

When you can key 15–20 *wam* above your 1' *gwam* rate for 15", increase the timings to 30". Move to the next line when you are able to complete at least 2 lines within the 30".

PRACTICE MAKES PERFECT

Set the Timer for 15 seconds. Key at least ten 15" timings, beginning on a line that is approximately 1/4 of your 1' *gwam* rate. Move to the next line when you are able to complete a line within 15". Force your stroking speed to a higher level on each timing.

1   She may pay them to work.
2   Alan is to go downtown by bus.
3   I may tow the big dock to the lake.
4   The official kept the dog by the kennel.
5   Pamela works in the coalfield for a neighbor.
6   Leith may sign the usual proxy for the city audit.
7   He may pay for the work on an emblem of the big chapel.

15" | 4 | 8 | 12 | 16 | 20 | 24 | 28 | 32 | 36 | 40 | 44 |

CONTROL GOAL

When you can key at 15–20 *wam* above your 1' *gwam* rate for 30", drop back two lines. Try to key that line with not more than one error for 30". Move to the next line when your control goal is met.

GRAMMAR CORNER

Study the spelling and definitions of the words below. Key the Learn line, noting the word choices. Key the Apply lines, selecting the correct words.

one   *(adjective) being a single thing*
won   *(verb) gain victory in a contest*

LEARN 1   He scored more than **one** point in each game we **won**.
APPLY 2   We (one, won) the game by (one, won) point.
APPLY 3   Sara scored (one, won) point, but we (one, won).

GRAMMAR CORNER

Read the punctuation rules below. Study the Learn lines. Note how the rules are applied. Compose one sentence (in longhand) for each rule, applying the rule.

Use a period at the end of a declarative sentence (a sentence that is not a question or exclamation).

LEARN 1   Here is your new dress.

LEARN 2   Please be home before 10 p.m.

Use a question mark at the end of a sentence intended as a question.

LEARN 3   Is that a new dress?

LEARN 4   Do you know what time your curfew is?

Use an exclamation point after an emphatic (forceful) exclamation.

LEARN 5   I really like your new dress!

LEARN 6   You were supposed to be home two hours ago!

KEYING ON YOUR OWN

Key each line twice SS (slowly, then faster). DS between 2-line groups.

3rd-Row Emphasis

1   to is so are rut dug hut too tear dear here sister
2   wear idol odor usher reuse trust ideal offer ultra
3   she is to go; he owes two; it is low; he is three;

1st-Row Emphasis

4   can an call calf and hand cash sack clan nasal canal
5   Canada clan class fang lack hang flank gangs gland
6   a fan; a hand; a can; an ad; an ash; cash a; and a

All Letters Learned

7   Doug and Fran left on a walk to get cans of juice.
8   Jack walked one hour; Nita got to walk four hours.
9   Sarah left to swing. Jackie is scheduled for two.

THINKING CAP

Using just the keys at the right, key as many U.S. state names as you can. Remember, key the states using only the letters at the right.

a   c   d   e   f   g   h   i   j   k   l   n   o   r   s   t   u   w
Right Shift and Left Shift

The Paragraph dialog box and the margin markers on the Ruler can be used to set special paragraph indents. You can indent the first line of the paragraph(s) or all lines except the first line. Both settings can be useful when keying reports.

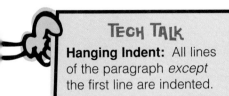

TECH TALK

Hanging Indent: All lines of the paragraph *except* the first line are indented.

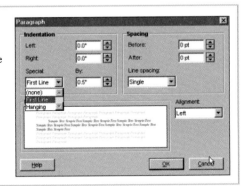

COMPUTER WIZ

Move just the top part of the left margin marker to create a first line indent for a paragraph. Move just the bottom part of the left margin marker to create a hanging indent.

Learn to Set Paragraph Indents

1. Select the paragraph(s) you wish to indent. Click *Format* on the Menu bar. Click *Paragraph*. The Paragraph dialog box appears.

2. Click the down arrow for the Special Indentation drop-down box and click *First Line* or *Hanging*. Key a number (in inches) in the By box to indicate the amount of the indent.

3. Click *OK* to close the dialog box.

First Line Indent. This paragraph has a first line indent of 0.5". This indent is appropriate for paragraphs in a report that is double spaced.

Hanging Indent. This paragraph has a hanging indent of 0.5". This indent is appropriate for reference items.

Practice What You Have Learned

1. Open **L33Margins** if it is not already open.

2. For Paragraphs 1, 2, and 3, indent the first line 0.75".

3. Below Paragraph 5, key the two paragraphs shown below.

   <u>The Information Please Almanac</u>. "Large Lakes of the World." Boston: Houghton Mifflin Company, 1994.

   <u>The World Almanac and Book of Facts</u>. "Major Natural Lakes of the World." Mahwah, NJ: World Almanac Books, 1999.

4. Set a 0.5" hanging indent for Paragraphs 6 and 7 (shown above).

5. Save the document as **L33Indents**.

LESSON 12

b and p

CASEY'S WARM UP

Key each line twice SS (once slowly, then again at a faster pace). DS between 2-line groups.

1 code got ask for hits just lunch two cash not cast
2 goes to|as he|down town|and juice|for golf|kind of
3 The grown kid drank his juice after the last race.

PRACTICE MAKES PERFECT

Key each line twice. DS between 2-line groups. Keep your eyes on the textbook as you key.

Practice b
1 fb fb bf bf be be bib bib big big but but bit bit;
2 boat beat bite bear bare bath bake best blob batch
3 too big; be back; belt it; big blue book; big bear

Practice p
4 ;p ;p p; p; pa pa pep pep put put pen pen pop pop;
5 pear peer peep part page pint pour pure pier print
6 papers proper purple puppet propel prepaid prepare

Practice b and p
7 apt bat pin bit sap tub tip bus pat bean part bale
8 bats past base pass burps bribe paper pride burlap
9 paper plate; bat and ball; punt or pass; baseballs

3. The left and right margin settings are indicated on the Ruler by the left and right margin markers.

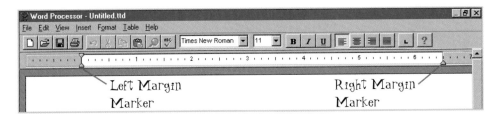

Practice What You Have Learned

1. Open a new document. Set the left and right margins so each is 2".

2. Key the paragraph shown below after Step 8.

3. Make four copies of the text, placing each a double-space beneath the other. You should have a total of five paragraphs.

4. Place the insertion point within the second paragraph and change the left and right margins to 1.5". *Notice that only the margins of the second paragraph change.*

5. Select (highlight) Paragraphs 3 and 4 and change the left and right margins to 0.5". *Notice that the margin change applies to both paragraphs because both were selected.*

6. Change the left and right margins of Paragraph 5 to 1.75".

7. Set the top margin to 2" and the bottom margin to 0.75".

8. Save the document as **L33Margins**.

I am changing the left and right margins so I can use different line lengths. I can make these changes in the Page Settings dialog box or by moving the margin markers on the Ruler.

To change the side margins using the Ruler, drag *both* the top and bottom parts of the left margin marker or the *single* right margin marker on the Ruler. Hold down the *Alt* key while dragging the bottom marker to move the left margin.

Drag Left Margin Marker

Key each line twice SS (slowly, then faster). DS between 2-line groups.

3rd-Row Emphasis

1 part opal usual right like ropes paper plate swats
2 rip opera throat sweater were supper fighter issue
3 to put; he is; of us; is low; if we put; to supper

All Letters Learned

4 Jack and Doug left before Wes shipped the product.
5 Charles used to work for the big shop in San Juan.
6 Patti took a bus downhill; Cal gets a jet at four.

WRITING CORNER

Think about your favorite movie star. Write notes in longhand recording the information you know about the star. Organize the information in a logical order in outline format.

Draft a paragraph or two (in longhand) about the movie star. Edit the paragraph(s) to make sure your message is clear and correct. Give the completed assignment to your teacher.

THINKING CAP

Key each sentence at the right. Choose a state capital from those shown at the top to correctly complete each sentence.

Atlanta	Lansing
Baton Rouge	Little Rock
Honolulu	Raleigh
Indianapolis	Springfield
Juneau	Tallahassee

The capital of Alaska is _____.

The capital of Arkansas is _____.

The capital of Florida is _____.

The capital of Georgia is _____.

The capital of North Carolina is _____.

Key each line once. DS between each set of lines.

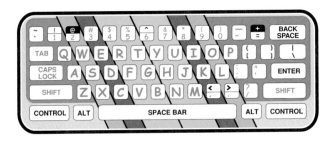

Practice @ (at sign)

1 s @ s @ s@ S@ s@s S@s @s@ @s@ My e-mail is dexterj@emi.

2 E-mail Jim at jimford@fti.org and Jan at jan77@jti.com.

Practice + (plus sign)

3 ; + ; + ;+ ;+ ;+; ;+; +;+ I can add 45+55+100 mentally.

4 Ken added 44+55+66 and Kim added 55+24+34 very quickly.

Practice @ and +

5 Send the picture to Viv+1@home.com and Kit+Jim@eti.org.

6 Mia's recent invoice listed 7 doz. donuts @ 4.95/dozen.

WORD PROCESSING

MARGINS

The amount of blank space at the left and right edges (margins) of the paper can be adjusted so different line lengths can be used. The top and bottom margins can also be adjusted.

Learn to Set Margins

1. Click *Format* on the Menu bar. Click *Page Settings*. The Page Settings dialog box appears.

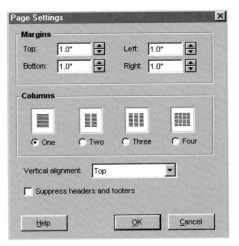

2. Key the desired measurements (in inches) in the Top, Bottom, Left, and Right text boxes. Click *OK*.

(continued on next page)

LESSON 13

Review

CASEY'S WARM UP

Key each line twice SS (once slowly, then again at a faster pace). DS between 2-line groups.

1   none ask juice drip free get lost two price brown;
2   just in case|a cup of|the black dog|at work|for it
3   Buford knows it is his job to take the golden cup.

WORD PROCESSING

TIMER

Use the Timer feature when you key timed writings. The Timer "counts" the amount of time you indicate and displays the timing results.

COMPUTER WIZ

Click the *Timer* button to display the Timer dialog box or to stop a timing.

Using the Timer

1. Click *Edit* on the Menu bar. Click *Timer*. The Timer dialog box appears.

2. Click the *Count-down timer* option if it is not already selected.

3. Click the desired time or key a time in the Variable minutes or seconds box.

4. Click *OK*. The time indicated in the Timer dialog box appears on the lower-right corner of the screen and counts down during the timing.

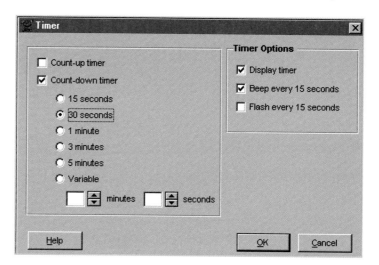

(continued on next page)

Keyboarding Enrichment and Review @ and +

CASEY'S WARM UP

Key each line twice SS (once slowly, then again at a faster pace). DS between 2-line groups.

1   Jo is amazed how quickly a proud man fixed the big van.
2   We have stores at 396 Elm, 1802 Palm, and 4507 Hartley.
3   Nancy and I may sign the proxy if we make a firm audit.

PRACTICE MAKES PERFECT

Key each line twice SS (once slowly, then again at a faster pace). DS between 2-line groups.

TECHNIQUE TIP
Keep hands and arms quiet and wrists low. Do not read too far in advance of keying.

Home/First Row

1   ax am an sac man ban van bag zinc nail ball mink and/or
2   a.m./p.m., van and car, fox or mink, zebras and/or mink
3   men buzz navy women comic babbles mnemonic names velvet

Double Letters

4   see inn all boon will effort funny boost deepen furrier
5   soon tall utter upper swoon flurry accrue bubble assess
6   illegal boon food hill puppy skill little rubber smooth

GRAMMAR CORNER

Study the spelling and definitions of the words below. Key the Learn line, noting the word choices. Key the Apply lines, selecting the correct words.

weak	*(adjective) lacking strength or vigor*
week	*(noun) seven successive days*
LEARN 1	We played a **weak** team last **week**.
APPLY 2	He grew (weak, week) in the past (weak, week).
APPLY 3	Andy was the (weak, week) link this (weak, week).

TECH TALK

A **standard word** in keyboarding is any combination of 5 characters and spaces. The standard words keyed in 1' is called gross words a minute (*gwam*).

TECH TALK

You cannot edit a timing document after closing the Timing Results dialog box. You can, however, print or save the timing document, key another timing (press *Ctrl+1*), or open a new document to start other work.

5. The Timer starts counting down the time when you strike a key. When the time has elapsed, the Timing Results dialog box appears. The elapsed time, the number of words keyed, and the gross words a minute (*gwam*) are shown in the dialog box.

6. Review the timed writing results and click *OK* to close the dialog box.

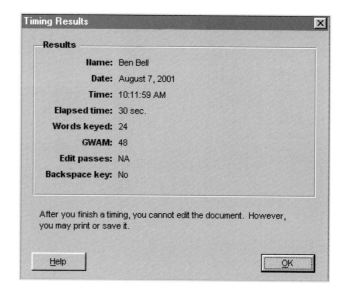

PRACTICE MAKES PERFECT

Set the Timer for 30 seconds. Key each line for 30 seconds, trying to complete the line before the time elapses. If you complete the line, strike *Enter/Return* and key the line again. Keep your eyes on the textbook as you key.

1 Dick has an old truck to sell.
2 Ben will be in town this week.

3 Jackie could be on the first train.
4 Greg took his boat to the big lake.

5 Jessica took the truck down to the dock.
6 It took the train longer than I thought.

7 I think Jorge will be able to go before noon.
8 The golfing class will not start until April.

30" | 2 | 4 | 6 | 8 | 10 | 12 | 14 | 16 | 18 |

TECH TALK

To take additional timings, press *Ctrl+1*. (Do not save the timings unless instructed to do so.)

Tabs you set can be cleared (removed) individually or all at once.

COMPUTER WIZ

To clear a tab using the Ruler, click the tab marker on the Ruler and drag it off the bottom of the Ruler.

TECH TALK

Tab changes apply to the current paragraph (the paragraph that contains the insertion point). If multiple paragraphs are selected, the changes will apply to the selected paragraphs.

Learn to Clear Tabs

1. Select the paragraph(s) for which you want to clear (delete) tabs.

2. Click *Format* on the Menu bar. Click *Tabs*. In the Tabs dialog box, click *Clear All* to clear all the tabs you have set.

3. To clear a single tab, select the tab position in the Tabs dialog box and click *Clear*.

4. Click *OK* to close the dialog box.

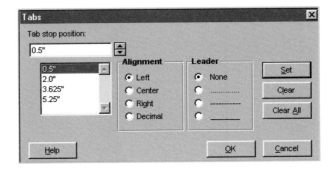

Practice What You Have Learned

1. Open a new document. Set a left tab at 1", center tabs at 2.75" and 4.5", and a right tab at 6". Key the text below in a bold font using the tabs just set.

Room	Name	Amount	Place

2. Place the insertion point on the line below the keyed text. Clear the center tab at 4.5" by dragging it from the Ruler.

3. Set a decimal tab at 4.5". Key the three lines of text below in a regular font using the tabs just set.

101	Jim Car	$127.55	First
218	Bev Oats	$79.85	Second
12	Jill Lockitt	$67.35	Third

4. Make a copy of the lines and place the copy a double-space below the original.

5. In the copy, select all the lines and use the Tabs dialog box to clear all the tabs.

6. Save the document as **L32Tabs**.

GRAMMAR CORNER

Study the definitions of the words below and the Learn lines. Note the correct way to use the words. Compose one sentence (in longhand) using the word "no" and another sentence using the word "know."

no   (adverb/adjective/noun) not in any respect or degree; not so; indicates denial or refusal

know   (verb) to be aware of the truth of; to have understanding of

LEARN 1   She said **no** to my request.

LEARN 2   **No**, you are not eligible for the scholarship.

LEARN 3   Did you **know** the answer?

LEARN 4   I did not **know** that you were going too.

KEYING ON YOUR OWN

Key each line twice SS (slowly, then faster). DS between 2-line groups.

Space Bar Emphasis

1   Gene saw the old dog up at the lake near the dock.

2   Joan left soon after I got to the top of the hill.

3   Chan will be here soon to talk to the entire club.

Shift Key Emphasis

4   Carlos and Rebecca went to see Edgardo and Ichiro.

5   LaCrosse and Wauwatosa are two towns in Wisconsin.

6   Erika Chi and Logan Ash took a bus to Los Angeles.

THINKING CAP

Unscramble the letters shown at the right to create the names of ten U.S. presidents. After you key the names, list the presidents in the order they served as president, going from first to last.

trreaC	nnlLcio
huBs	angeRa
dogelioC	ffneorsJe
gthsWnnaoi	tnraG
oFdr	atfT

GRAMMAR CORNER

Study the spelling and definitions of the words below. Key the Learn line, noting the word choices. Key the Apply lines, selecting the correct words.

to	(preposition) in the direction of; at, on, or near
too	(adverb) in addition, also, beyond
two	(noun) one more than one

LEARN 1   I, **too**, hope **to** view **two** movies this weekend.
APPLY 2   Are you (to, too, two) going (to, too, two) go with me?
APPLY 3   It's (to, too, two) much to hope for (to, too, two) pieces.

KEYING ON YOUR OWN: REVIEW _ AND *

Key each line once. DS between each set of lines.

UNDERLINE TIP

When consecutive words are underlined, the space between them is usually underlined to increase efficiency.

Practice _ (underline)

1   ; _ ; _ ;_ ;_ ;_ ;_ _;_   Underline <u>sixteen</u> and <u>eight</u>.
2   <u>Truth</u>, <u>honesty</u>, and <u>respect</u> are key words in the motto.

Practice * (asterisk/multiply)

3   k * k * k* k* k*k k*k *k* An * tells Naomi to multiply.
4   New fares have an *, thus: $8*, $9*, and $49* are new.

Practice _ and *

5   Mark all words in <u>red</u>, <u>blue</u>, <u>green</u>, and <u>pink</u> with an *.
6   <u>Chin Lu's</u> problem is 127*508 and <u>Jon Dean's</u> is 439*196.

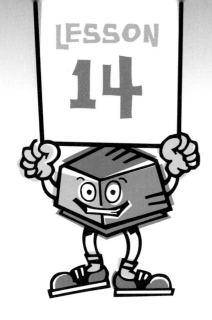

LESSON 14

m and x

CASEY'S WARM UP

Key each line twice SS (once slowly, then again at a faster pace). DS between 2-line groups.

1 of as de fg jh ki lo ;p we fr tf cd jn be ge ka dl
2 no ice bat sub dog the jet kit lot rat was due pet
3 Dean will pick up the bag with juice after school.

PRACTICE MAKES PERFECT

Key each line twice. DS between 2-line groups. Keep your eyes on the textbook as you key.

Practice m
1 jm jm me me met met meat meat make make more more;
2 mjmj mat mat men men ment ment memo memo mold mold
3 moms moms mumps mumps summer summer emblem emblem;

Practice x
4 s x s x six six fix fix box box ox ox extra extra;
5 xs xs exit exit excel excel fax fax excite excite;
6 an ox; a fox; a box; at six; to mix; to fix the ax

Practice m and x
7 mm xx mx mx xm xm me jam six fix mix box memo Lexi
8 six mean men; next memo; extra map; mix and match;
9 Sam can mix a ham salad; Max can fix soup for six.

LESSON 32

Keyboarding Enrichment and Review _ and *

CASEY'S WARM UP

Key each line twice SS (once slowly, then again at a faster pace). DS between 2-line groups.

1 Muffy saw an extra jet quickly zip over the big desert.
2 Of 2,304 students taking the test, 1,896 passed at 75%.
3 Six girls in the dorm may handle half of the endowment.

PRACTICE MAKES PERFECT

Set the Timer for 1 minute. Key at least two 1' timings on each paragraph. Then key two 2' writings on both paragraphs. Determine *gwam* and errors.

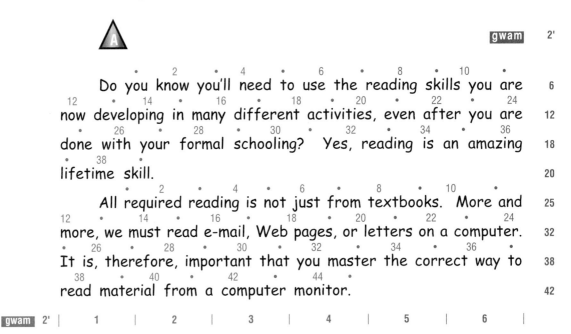

A

gwam | 2'

| | • | 2 | • | 4 | • | 6 | • | 8 | • | 10 | • | |
Do you know you'll need to use the reading skills you are | 6
12 | • | 14 | • | 16 | • | 18 | • | 20 | • | 22 | • | 24
now developing in many different activities, even after you are | 12
 • | 26 | • | 28 | • | 30 | • | 32 | • | 34 | • | 36 |
done with your formal schooling? Yes, reading is an amazing | 18
 • | 38 |
lifetime skill. | 20

| | • | 2 | • | 4 | • | 6 | • | 8 | • | 10 | • |
All required reading is not just from textbooks. More and | 25
12 | • | 14 | • | 16 | • | 18 | • | 20 | • | 22 | • | 24
more, we must read e-mail, Web pages, or letters on a computer. | 32
 • | 26 | • | 28 | • | 30 | • | 32 | • | 34 | • | 36 | •
It is, therefore, important that you master the correct way to | 38
 38 | • | 40 | • | 42 | • | 44 | • |
read material from a computer monitor. | 42

gwam 2' | 1 | 2 | 3 | 4 | 5 | 6 |

GRAMMAR CORNER

Read the comma rules below. Study the Learn lines. Compose one sentence (in longhand) for each rule, applying the rule.

Use a comma after introductory phrases or clauses.

LEARN 1   When you finish taking the exam, please turn it in.
LEARN 2   If you go to the school dance, Dana would like to go too.

Use a comma after words in a series.

LEARN 3   The play will be held on Tuesday, Wednesday, and Thursday.
LEARN 4   Pictures of Felipe, Anne, and Carlos were on the cover.

Use a comma before short direct quotations.

LEARN 5   The woman asked, "When is the next flight to Atlanta?"
LEARN 6   Mark shouted, "I got an A on the final exam!"

KEYING ON YOUR OWN

Set the Timer for 30 seconds. Key each line for 30 seconds. If you complete the line, strike *Enter/Return* and key the line again.

1   Sarah has the book Hal wanted.
2   Jo will call her next weekend.

3   Jorge beat the game the first time.
4   Susan ran two more miles last week.

5   Allan left his hat and coat on the rock.
6   Doug put the computer back in the chest.

7   Oksana arranged to meet Angie after the show.
8   Their next golf match will not start on time.

30" | 2 | 4 | 6 | 8 | 10 | 12 | 14 | 16 | 18 |

THINKING CAP

Key each sentence shown at the right. Choose a state capital from the list below to complete each sentence correctly.

Bismarck   Lincoln
Columbia   Madison
Columbus   Pierre
Des Moines   St. Paul
Jackson   Topeka

The capital of Iowa is _____.
The capital of Kansas is _____.
The capital of Minnesota is _____.
The capital of Nebraska is _____.
The capital of South Dakota is _____.

The Word Processor has left tabs already set at half-inch (0.5") intervals from the left margin. These default tabs do not have tab markers on the Ruler. Left, center, right, and decimal tabs may be set anywhere on the Ruler. **Left** *tabs align text at the left.* **Right** *tabs align text at the right.* **Center** *tabs center text on the tab position.* **Decimal** *tabs center text at the decimal point.*

Learn to Set Tabs

1. Click *Format* on the Menu bar. Click *Tabs*. The Tabs dialog box appears.

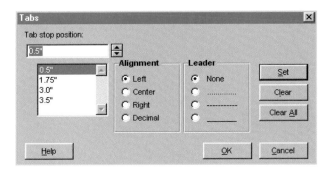

2. Key a number for the Tab stop in the Tab stop position box. Click an Alignment option (Left, Center, Right, Decimal). Click *Set*. Repeat for all tabs you wish to set.

3. Click *OK* to close the dialog box. A tab marker appears on the Ruler for each tab you set. (Default tabs to the left of any set tab are deleted automatically.)

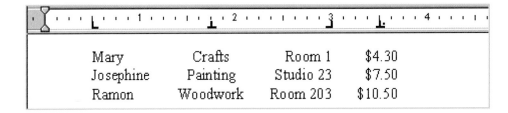

Practice What You Have Learned

1. Open a new document. Set a left tab at 1", a center tab at 2.5", a decimal tab at 3.75", and a right tab at 5.25". Key the text below using the tabs just set.

Room 101	Jim Car	$127.55	First Place
Room 218	Bev Oats	$79.85	Second Place
Room 12	Jill Lockitt	$67.35	Third Place

2. Save the document as **L31Tabs**.

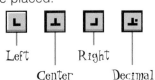

To set a tab using the toolbar, click the *Tab Style* button on the toolbar to select a tab style. Click the Ruler at the position the new tab is to be placed.

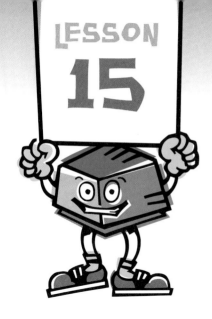

LESSON 15

y and z

CASEY'S WARM UP

Key each line twice SS (once slowly, then again at a faster pace). DS between 2-line groups.

1 pa to if up as do no ax am an or be he go it we us
2 orange juice|it will|be here|of our|ice cold water
3 Katie was excited about the next trip to the lake.

PRACTICE MAKES PERFECT

Key each line twice. DS between 2-line groups. Keep your eyes on the textbook as you key.

Practice y

1 jy jay jay joy joy yes yes yards yards yield yield
2 yet yet say say hay hay may may bay bay days days;
3 nay or yea; you may; truly yours; many days; I say

Practice z

4 azaz zip zip zoo zoo zero zero haze haze zoom zoom
5 zinc zinc zone zone daze daze maze maze zeal zeal
6 to zigzag; the zoo; too dizzy; real cozy; too lazy

Practice y and z

7 y z zy joy zany you lazy boy crazy yard hazy happy
8 an eye; to zip; you are; speed zone; amazing years
9 Liz was puzzled by the lazy boy and the crazy pup.

GRAMMAR CORNER

Read the number usage rule below. Key the Learn line, noting the number choices. Key the Apply lines, making the necessary corrections.

Spell indefinite numbers.

LEARN 1   Almost sixty classmates are going.
APPLY 2   Nearly 75 schools will field teams this year.
APPLY 3   Approximately 50 students passed.

KEYING ON YOUR OWN: REVIEW ' AND "

Key each line once. DS between each set of lines.

Practice ' (apostrophe)

1   ; ' ; ' ;' ;' ;'; ;'; ';' Is this Kit's?   No it's Jim's.
2   If I can't go, I'll call Jack's house if it's not late.

Practice " (quotation mark)

3   ; " ; " ;" ;" ;"; ;"; ";"   "See you there," Jackie said.
4   Use "choose" instead of "chose"; "by" instead of "buy."

Practice ' and "

5   Renee' asked me if "The Early Years" is a good magazine.
6   Ms. O'Brien asked Mrs. O'Neil, "Why can't my class go?"

WRITING CORNER

Alexander Graham Bell
Thomas Edison
Christopher Sholes
Benjamin Franklin
George Washington
 Carver
Walter E. Disney
Henry Ford
Orville and Wilbur Wright

A list of famous inventors is shown at the left. Search the Internet (or other reference sources) to learn about one of these individuals.

Take notes in longhand, recording the information you learn from your sources. Review the notes and choose the most important information about the inventor. Organize the information in a logical order in outline format.

Draft a paragraph or two (in longhand) about the inventor. Edit the paragraph(s) to make sure your message is clear and correct. Give the completed assignment to your teacher.

KEYING ON YOUR OWN

Key each line twice SS (slowly, then faster). DS between 2-line groups.

1st/3rd Rows

1 zoo yet noon nice roper moon top cop boy exit were
2 Elizabeth Martinez may be on their team next year.

Space Bar Emphasis

3 a be he is old can she you top we rat zap cat exam
4 James may be able to help with the next bake sale.

Key Phrases

5 it will be | if you are | may be able | there is a | it is
6 to be able | this is the | could be | if you can | soon as

THINKING CAP

Key each sentence shown at the top right. Choose a state from the list below to complete each sentence correctly.

California   Maine
Delaware   New York
Florida   Rhode Island
Kansas   Utah

The smallest state in the United States is _____.

The state that grows the most wheat is _____.

The state where people see the sun rise first is _____.

The state with the largest population is _____.

The first state in the United States was _____.

Keyboarding Enrichment and Review ' and "

CASEY'S WARM UP

Key each line twice SS (once slowly, then again at a faster pace). DS between 2-line groups.

1 Before leaving, Jess quickly swam the dozen extra laps.
2 Order 19068 was for 38 vests, 72 shirts, and 45 skirts.
3 The airmen got the visual signals to turn to the right.

ENDURANCE GOAL
When you can key 15–20 *wam* above your 1' *gwam* rate for 15", increase the timings to 30". Move to the next line when you are able to complete at least 2 lines within the 30".

PRACTICE MAKES PERFECT

Set the Timer for 15 seconds. Key at least ten 15" timings, beginning on a line that is approximately 1/4 of your 1' *gwam* rate. Move to the next line when you are able to complete a line within 15". Force your stroking speed to a higher level on each timing.

CONTROL GOAL
When you can key at 15–20 *wam* above your 1' *gwam* rate for 30", drop back two lines. Try to key that line with not more than one error for 30". Move to the next line when your control goal is met.

1 I may dismantle the jeep.
2 Jan and Lana may go with them.
3 I paid the man for the work he did.
4 The big problem is with the turn signal.
5 Pam is to work downtown for the city auditor.
6 Nancy got paid for the work she did on the shanty.
7 Pamela may go to the big sorority social on the island.

15" | 4 | 8 | 12 | 16 | 20 | 24 | 28 | 32 | 36 | 40 | 44 |

LESSON 16

q and comma (,)

CASEY'S WARM UP

Key each line twice SS (once slowly, then again at a faster pace). DS between 2-line groups.

1   July up gas tax cars bath not zoom make wait deaf;
2   a hazy day; extra lazy boy; is dizzy; zero degrees
3   Jackie said the family grew up near the Bronx Zoo.

PRACTICE MAKES PERFECT

Key each line twice. DS between 2-line groups. Keep your eyes on the textbook as you key.

Practice q

1   a q a q aq aqua aqua quay quay quit quit quip quip
2   quilt quartz quote squad quiet quack quick quarter
3   a quiz; to quit; a quote; quite quick; end quickly

Practice , (comma)

4   k , k , ,k, ,k, Please ask Tom, Mary, Ken, and me.
5   a day, a day; a man, a man; a bike, a bike; a band
6   Dan, Sam, and I can go; Jo, Sue, and Janet may go.

Practice q and ,

7   Quin Quigly, not Quin Quil, quickly took the quiz.
8   Quint, A, S, D, and F are the left hand home keys.
9   Quinton, Raquel, and Duque quickly quit the squad.

1. Key the copy below to create a flyer to be printed on 8.5" x 11" paper.

2. Use the paragraph alignments shown.

3. Choose the line spacing, font, font size, font style, font color, and other design elements to make an attractive flyer.

Harriet Tubman Middle School

5th Annual School Clean-up Day

May 15, 200-

9 a.m. to 2 p.m.

Middle School Auditorium

Safety vests, liter bags, and other supplies will be provided.

Refreshments and supervision provided by HTPTO.

Visit http://www.tubman.edu for more information.

This event is sponsored by the Student Council.

WRITING CORNER

Search the Internet (or other reference sources) to learn about your favorite musician, sports celebrity, scientist, or other well-known public figure. Using your search results, compose a paragraph that provides information about the person and his or her accomplishments. Save the document as **L30Person**.

© PhotoDisc, Inc.

GRAMMAR CORNER

Study the definitions of the words below and the Learn lines. Note the correct use of the words. Compose one sentence (in longhand) using the word "for" and another sentence using the word "four."

for   *(preposition/conjunction) used to indicate purpose; on behalf of; because; because of*

four   *(adjective/noun) totaling one more than three; the number between three and five*

LEARN 1   I will attend the meeting **for** Mr. Sanchez.
LEARN 2   Jason will only be there **for** an hour.

LEARN 3   Kellee had **four** teeth pulled on Thursday.
LEARN 4   Kammi played the **four** of hearts.

KEYING ON YOUR OWN

Set the Timer for 30 seconds. Key each line for 30 seconds. If you complete the line, strike *Enter/Return* and key the line again.

1   Space quickly after each word.
2   Then, quickly key another one.

3   Do not look at the keys as you key.
4   Looking at the keys slows you down.

5   Try to key a little faster on each line.
6   You need to force yourself to go faster.

7   A person can key much faster than she writes.
8   Writing words in longhand takes a lot longer.

30" | 2 | 4 | 6 | 8 | 10 | 12 | 14 | 16 | 18 |

Read the number usage rule below. Key the Learn lines, noting number choices. Key the Apply lines, making the necessary corrections.

Use figures for a series of fractions but spell isolated fractions.

LEARN 1   Amy's share was 1/4 on Monday and 2/3 on Tuesday.
LEARN 2   Amy made two-thirds of the cookies.
APPLY 3   My answers are five-sixths, one-third, and one-half.
APPLY 4   I got 60 answers correct; that is 4/5.

KEYING ON YOUR OWN: REVIEW (AND)

Key each line once. DS between each set of lines.

SPACING TIP
Do not space between (and) and the copy they enclose.

Practice ((left parenthesis)

1   l (l (l((l((l9 (l9 (9 (9 Use the l finger to key (.
2   He reaches quickly with the l finger to key 9 or the (.

Practice) (right parenthesis)

3   ;) ;) ;));))l0)l0)0)0 Use the ; finger to key).
4   He reaches quickly with the ; finger to key 0 or the).

Practice (and)

5   My text is from section II(B)(iv)(c) of the legal code.
6   Mara will be graduated in ('06); Juan ('08); Tim ('09).

*At the end of a full line, the text and insertion point move to the next line automatically. This is called **word wrap** (soft return). Use word wrap when you key a paragraph.*

Practice Word Wrap

Key the two paragraphs below using word wrap. At the end of a paragraph, strike *Enter/Return* twice (two hard returns) to place one blank line between paragraphs.

When you want to be better at something you cannot do as well as you wish, you keep practicing. You do not just repeat old actions; or if you do, you do not get better. Rather, you repeat the general response but with some change in the act.

The next time you are asked to do the drill again, try to use a better method. Try to make quick, precise motions and let your mind tell the fingers what to do.

THINKING CAP

Unscramble the letters at the right to create the names of ten U.S. presidents. Then list the presidents in the order they served as president, going from first to last.

showernEie	rangdiH
lilemroF	ledCnvael
nioWsl	xNnio
eennyKd	iMasndo
lokP	rlyTe

LESSON 30

Keyboarding Enrichment and Review (and)

CASEY'S WARM UP

Key each line twice SS (once slowly, then again at a faster pace). DS between 2-line groups.

1 Jackie will help Martezy fix the big, quaint old store.
2 She sold 23 at $450, 83 at $910 less 24%, & 16 at $759.
3 The busy auditor is to handle the problems when I work.

PRACTICE MAKES PERFECT

Key each line twice SS (once slowly, then again at a faster pace). DS between 2-line groups.

Shift-Lock

1 Carlie listens to stations WBEX-AM, KDKT-AM, or WMBO-AM.
2 CHI LEI finished first; SU LI second; SANDRA LOPES third.
3 He read OUTLOOK, THE WALL, and THE FIRST ATTEMPT.

Left-Hand Words

4 ad be car dad ear fad raw sad tea wet zab vat bags gets
5 fret area bear care dear ease face gate rave saga straw
6 set tact vest wage zest arts best cave deed fares great

> **TECHNIQUE TIP**
> Do not pause before or after striking the *CAPS LOCK* key. Keep your hands and arms quiet and your wrists low.

Review

CASEY'S WARM UP

Key each line twice SS (once slowly, then again at a faster pace). DS between 2-line groups.

1 Jason amazed Wes by escaping quickly from the box.
2 Josh went to San Diego, Santa Fe, and Los Angeles.
3 Shane may go to the city with me to buy a big box.

PRACTICE MAKES PERFECT

Key each paragraph once SS as shown. Do not use word wrap. Strike *Enter/Return* at the end of each line to insert a hard return. DS between paragraphs.

TECHNIQUE TIP

Keep your eyes on the textbook as you strike *Enter/Return*.

Paragraph 1

At the end of a line quickly strike the Enter key
SS
and immediately begin keying the next line. After
SS
you complete a paragraph, strike the Enter key twice.
DS

Paragraph 2

If you strike the Enter key twice, one blank line
SS
will be left between the paragraphs that are being
SS
keyed. This makes it easy to read the paragraphs.

Use the Line Spacing command to change the amount of white space between lines of text. Single spacing is the default line spacing. Other frequently used spacing options are 1.5 lines and double spacing.

COMPUTER WIZ

Line spacing can be changed before or after text is keyed. To change the line spacing of keyed text, select the desired paragraph(s) and then set the line spacing in the Paragraph dialog box.

Change Line Spacing

1. Place the insertion point on the line that is to be followed by the new line spacing.

2. Click *Format* on the Menu bar. Click *Paragraph*. The Paragraph dialog box appears.

3. Click the down arrow for the Line spacing drop-down list and click a spacing option. Click *OK*.

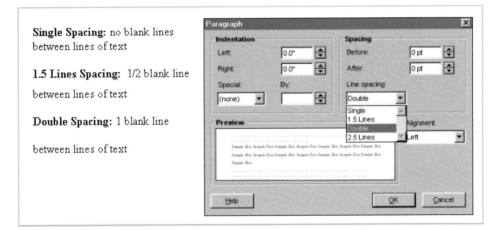

Single Spacing: no blank lines between lines of text

1.5 Lines Spacing: 1/2 blank line between lines of text

Double Spacing: 1 blank line between lines of text

Practice What You Have Learned

1. Set the line spacing to Double and the alignment to Center. Key the information requested below.

   Your name
   Name of your teacher
   Name of your school

2. Make two copies of the text. Place each copy a quadruple-space below the other.

3. Change the line spacing of the first copy to Single.

4. Change the line spacing of the second copy to 1.5 Lines.

GRAMMAR CORNER

Read the comma rules below. Study the Learn lines. Compose one sentence (in longhand) for each rule, applying the rule.

Use a comma before and after a word or words in apposition (words that come together and refer to the same person or thing).

LEARN 1   Marshall, the flight attendant, left his coat on the plane.
LEARN 2   The manager, Martin Furcal, will meet with us.

Use a comma to set off words of direct address (the name of a person spoken to).

LEARN 3   I believe, Mary, that the information is confidential.
LEARN 4   Please let me know, Mr. Boggs, if I can help.

Use a comma to separate the day from the year and the city from the state.

LEARN 5   Kenneth moved to Denver on July 4, 1998.
LEARN 6   Sandra was born in San Francisco, California.

KEYING ON YOUR OWN

Set the Timer for 30 seconds. Key each line for 30 seconds. If you complete the line, strike *Enter/Return* and key the line again.

1   He may be here in a day or so.
2   He will take the biology test.

3   He went to the dock to look for it.
4   She just left for the bank at noon.

5   They want to be in town for the holiday.
6   There will be just two of us on the bus.

7   Please buy me one of those hats for the game.
8   He baked two cakes for the next office party.

30" | 2 | 4 | 6 | 8 | 10 | 12 | 14 | 16 | 18 |

| Albany | Augusta | Concord | Hartford | Jefferson City |
| Annapolis | Boston | Frankfort | Helena | Trenton |

The capital of Maine is _____.
The capital of Massachusetts is _____.
The capital of New Hampshire is _____.
The capital of New Jersey is _____.

THINKING CAP

Key each sentence shown at the right. Choose a state capital from the list at the top to complete each sentence correctly.

GRAMMAR CORNER

Read the number usage rule below. Key the Learn line, noting number choices. Key the Apply lines, making the necessary corrections.

Spell (capitalized) names of small-numbered streets and avenues (ten and under).

LEARN 1   My house is located at 15 Fifth Ave. and 33rd Street.
APPLY 2   We will bike from First St. to Fifteenth Street.
APPLY 3   Sue moved from 2nd Avenue to 65th Street.

KEYING ON YOUR OWN: REVIEW # AND &

Key each line once. DS between each set of lines.

SPACING TIP
Do not space between # and a figure.

Space once before and after & used to join names.

Do not space before & in initials.

Practice # (number/pounds)

1   d # d # d# #d# #d3 #d3 #3 Shift fast to key #3 and #33.
2   He purchased items numbered #345, #678, #901 and #421.

Practice & (ampersand)

3   j & j & j7 &j& &j7 &j7 &7 We shopped at Holmes & Leone.
4   Key & in initials without a space, as in B&O, A&M, C&I.

Practice # and &

5   The # represents number and pounds. Jane weighed 115#.
6   IBO&AX bought 50# of #3 apples at GT&O on account #764.

LESSON 18

v and colon (:)

CASEY'S WARM UP

Key each line twice SS (once slowly, then again at a faster pace). DS between 2-line groups.

1 Glen James quickly packed two boxes of the prizes.
2 to buy | it is | here are | of it | to be able | you will be
3 I may go to the small island town by the big lake.

PRACTICE MAKES PERFECT

Key each line twice. DS between 2-line groups. Keep your eyes on the textbook as you key.

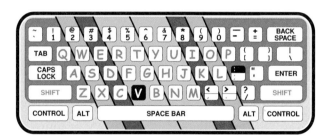

Practice v

1 f v f v vi vi vie vie vet vet five five vain vain;
2 ivy live very avail pave save vine ever favor vote
3 very trivial; five flavors; ivy vines; seven votes

Practice : (colon)

4 ; ; ; : :: To: From: Date: Subject: To: From:
5 Dear Mr. Gonzalez: Dear Ms. Chi: Dear Ms. Sabin:
6 Space twice after a colon, thus: Try these steps:

Practice v and :

7 To: Vic Voss From: Vicky River Date: November
8 Three people will attend: Val, Villa, and Victor.
9 These are the winners: Vic Valdez and Vern Vance.

SPACING TIP
Space twice after : used as punctuation.

LESSON 29

Keyboarding Enrichment and Review # and &

CASEY'S WARM UP

Key each line twice SS (once slowly, then again at a faster pace). DS between 2-line groups.

1 Jim placed first by solving the complex quiz in a week.
2 A new van, #B928-754, is parked in Space 103 in Lot 16.
3 Did the firm bid for the authentic title to the island?

PRACTICE MAKES PERFECT

Set the Timer for 1 minute. Key at least two 1' timings on each paragraph. Then key two 2' timings on both paragraphs. Determine *gwam* and errors.

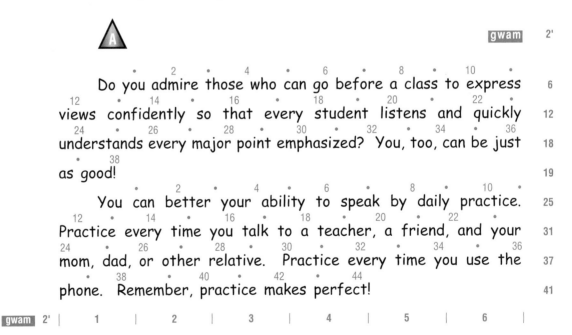

| | gwam | 2' |

Do you admire those who can go before a class to express 6
views confidently so that every student listens and quickly 12
understands every major point emphasized? You, too, can be just 18
as good! 19

You can better your ability to speak by daily practice. 25
Practice every time you talk to a teacher, a friend, and your 31
mom, dad, or other relative. Practice every time you use the 37
phone. Remember, practice makes perfect! 41

gwam 2' | 1 | 2 | 3 | 4 | 5 | 6 |

THINKING CAP

Key each sentence shown at the right. Choose a state capital from the list at the top right to complete each sentence correctly.

Boise   Oklahoma City
Carson City   Olympia
Cheyenne   Providence
Harrisburg   Sacramento
Montgomery   Salem

The capital of California is _____.

The capital of Idaho is _____.

The capital of Nevada is _____.

The capital of Oregon is _____.

The capital of Washington is _____.

KEYING ON YOUR OWN

Key each line twice SS (slowly, then faster). DS between 2-line groups.

Practice q and v

1 gave aqua have quit save quilt rave quiz oven quip
2 Vivian quit the quartet to move to Quincy to live.

Practice y and x

3 box buy fox cry six yes mix yet fix dry exact your
4 Mary Cox may give your extra yams to Barry Baxter.

Easy Sentences

5 Cody paid the girls for the signs they did for us.
6 The six busy men may go down to the field to work.

All Letters Learned

7 Jo Fox made five quick plays to win the big prize.
8 By solving the tax quiz, Jud Mack won first prize.

WRITING CORNER

Think about your favorite musician or musical group. Write notes in longhand recording the information you know about the person or group. Organize the information in a logical order in outline format.

Draft a paragraph or two (in longhand) about the person or group. Edit the paragraph(s) to make sure your message is clear and correct. Give the completed assignment to your teacher.

© PhotoDisc, Inc.

To change paragraph alignment quickly, click the *Align
Left*, *Align Center*, *Align
Right*, or *Justify* button on
the toolbar.

1. Using Right alignment, key your name. On the next line, key the current date.

2. Using Left alignment, key the name of your teacher on a new line. Key the name of your keyboarding course on the next line.

3. On a new line, key **A Trip to the Space Center** in an Arial, 16-point font. Change the alignment to Center.

4. On a new line in an Arial, 14-point font, key the paragraph. Change the alignment to Justified.

Student Name

Current Date

Teacher Name

Keyboarding I

A Trip to the Space Center

My favorite vacation was a trip to the beach. We played in the sand and collected shells. My brother found a star fish. I won a prize for the best sand castle on the beach.

LESSON 19

CAPS LOCK and question mark (?)

CASEY'S WARM UP

Key each line twice SS (once slowly, then again at a faster pace). DS between 2-line groups.

1 Jewel amazed Vic by escaping quickly from the box.
2 He may go | now and then | if she can | you can be | to be
3 He is to do social work for the city if they wish.

PRACTICE MAKES PERFECT

Key each line twice. DS between 2-line groups. Keep your eyes on the textbook as you key.

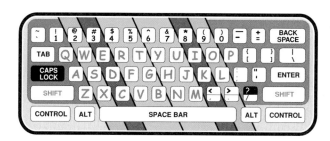

Practice CAPS LOCK

1 NBEA, DPE, and NAACP were the three organizations.
2 UCLA plays USC in the NCAA game televised on ESPN.
3 Terms for the next test include RAM, CPU, and ROM.

Practice ? (question mark)

4 ; ? ; ? ? ; Who? What? Where? When? Why? How?
5 Who is it? What is it? When is it? Where is it?
6 Did you go to the ballgame? Who played? Who won?

SPACING TIP
Space twice after a ? used as punctuation.

Key each line once. DS between each set of lines.

SPACING TIP

Do not space between a figure and %, nor before or after - (hyphen) or — (dash) used as punctuation.

Practice % (percent)

1 f % f % f% %f% %f5 %f5 8% 9% Just 60% will get 12% off.
2 Jane's best test scores are 75%, 86%, 91%, 84% and 92%.

Practice - (hyphen/minus)

3 ; - ; - ;- ;- ;-; ;-; 3-star James got a 5-star rating.
4 The combination to Jaye Reed-Todd's locker is 34-68-15.

Practice % and -

5 About 50% of the first-time students will come on 7-22.
6 About 60% of the riders take bus 61-A or 514-B to work.

WORD PROCESSING

PARAGRAPH ALIGNMENT

Paragraph alignment refers to the horizontal position of a paragraph of text. A paragraph is one or more lines that end with a hard return. Alignment options are Left, Center, Right, and Justified.

COMPUTER WIZ

To change alignment for existing paragraphs, click in a paragraph or select two or more paragraphs. Then set the alignment in the Paragraph dialog box.

Change Paragraph Alignment

To change paragraph alignment before the text is keyed:

1. Click *Format* on the Menu bar. Click *Paragraph*. The Paragraph dialog box appears.

2. Click the down arrow for the Alignment drop-down list box. Click on the desired alignment. Click *OK*.

Left Alignment: Lines are even at the left margin.

Center Alignment: Lines are centered between margins.

Right Alignment: Lines are even at the right margin.

Justified Alignment: Lines are even at the right and left margins.

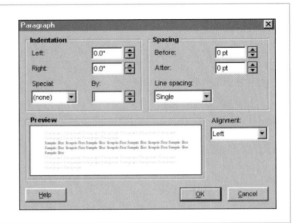

(continued on next page)

GRAMMAR CORNER

Study the definitions of the words below and the Learn lines. Note the correct use of the words. Compose one sentence (in longhand) using the word "your" and another sentence using the word "you're."

your   *(adjective) of or relating to you or yourself as possessor*

you're   *(contraction) you are*

LEARN 1   When is **your** book due?
LEARN 2   **Your** dad will pick you up in an hour.

LEARN 3   Please let me know when **you're** going to leave.
LEARN 4   **You're** supposed to call home immediately.

KEYING ON YOUR OWN

TIMING TIP
To find 1' *gwam*, add 10 for each line you completed to the scale figure beneath the point at which you stopped in a partial line. The total is your 1' *gwam*.

For lines 1–4, key each line twice SS (slowly, then faster). DS between 2-line groups. For lines 5–8, set the Timer for 1 minute. Key a 1' timed writing on each line; find *gwam* on each timing.

Key Words and Phrases

1   up car in be no sea noon sad moon feet pin are mop
2   you get set | was him | we are | no safe | as we | are extra
3   if when did pan dot rush ham man them pal fit lame
4   by the | to go to the | she kept it | he paid | the man is

Easy Sentences

5   Dick may go to the town to buy a box of the signs.
6   I did the work so the girls may go to town with us.
7   Jane may go with us to the city to sign the forms.
8   He may pay the firms for the work they did for us.

| gwam | 1' | 1 | 2 | 3 | 4 | 5 | 6 | 7 | 8 | 9 | 10 | |

LESSON 28

Keyboarding Enrichment and Review % and -

CASEY'S WARM UP

Key each line twice SS (once slowly, then again at a faster pace). DS between 2-line groups.

1 Zeb and Jaye gave a quick example of two helping verbs.
2 Both men risk a big penalty if they dismantle the auto.
3 Chrissie is to use numbers 105-44-33-5 and 178-66-32-5.

ENDURANCE GOAL
When you can key 15–20 *wam* above your 1' *gwam* rate for 15", increase the timings to 30". Move to the next line when you are able to complete at least 2 lines within the 30".

CONTROL GOAL
When you can key at 15–20 *wam* above your 1' *gwam* rate for 30", drop back two lines. Try to key that line with not more than one error for 30". Move to the next line when your control goal is met.

PRACTICE MAKES PERFECT

Set the Timer for 15 seconds. Key at least ten 15" timings, beginning on a line that is approximately 1/4 of your 1' *gwam* rate. Move to the next line when you are able to complete a line within 15". Force your stroking speed to a higher level on each timing.

1 Dorlena will go downtown.
2 He will work to fix the bugle.
3 Orlando may sign their audit forms.
4 The city has eighty auto firms downtown.
5 He and I may bid on the antique enamel bowls.
6 She is too busy to make the sign for the sorority.
7 A sick dog slept by the big oak chair in the dorm hall.

15" | 4 | 8 | 12 | 16 | 20 | 24 | 28 | 32 | 36 | 40 | 44 |

GRAMMAR CORNER

Read the number usage rule below. Key the Learn line, noting number choices. Key the Apply lines, making the necessary corrections.

Capitalize nouns preceding numbers (except page and line).

LEARN 1   Read lines 2-18 on page 33 in Chapter 2.
APPLY 2   Key lines 1-3 on Page 25.
APPLY 3   The law is stated in Section 1, Page 3, Line 5.

WRITING CORNER

Lesson 3: **Composers**
Lesson 6: **Baseball**
Lesson 9: **Artists**

Your teacher will return the paragraphs that you composed for Lessons 3, 6, and 9. Edit the paragraphs, making any additional changes that you wish. Key the paragraphs about each topic in a separate document and save them using the filenames shown at the left. You will use these files in completing a report in Lesson 40.

THINKING CAP

Unscramble the letters at the right to create the names of ten U.S. presidents. Then list the presidents in the order they served as president, going from first to last.

kycMenil

coanJsk

alrToy

syaHe

fadGlrie

vseooetlR

uranmT

rbVnnaue

eirmlloF

mdAsa

Key each line once. DS between each set of lines.

Practice / (diagonal/slash/divide)

1 ; / ; / ;/ /;/ /;? /;? 2/5 1/9 up/down Key 5/8 and 6/7.
2 Use 2/3 cup of milk and 1 1/2 cups of flour in the pie.

Practice $ (dollar)

3 f $ f $ f$ f $f4 $f4 $1 $3 $5 $7 Add $2, $4, and $90.
4 This week I collected $14, $23, $9, and $8 for charity.

Practice / and $

5 Web site http://www.rm.org/t was done in 8 1/2 hours.
6 I pay $10.95/month to subscribe to http://www.nesp.com.

SPACING TIP

Do not space between a figure and the / or $ sign.

WORD PROCESSING

APPLY WHAT YOU HAVE LEARNED

SPACING TIP

The **ellipsis** (. . .) shows the omission of words in text. Ellipsis points are three periods, each preceded and followed by a space.

1. Key the text shown below.
2. Place the title in a Times New Roman, 16-point font.
3. Arrange the eight attributes of being responsible in alphabetic order.
4. Display all text except the title in an Arial, 12-point font.
5. Display every other attribute in italic, beginning with the first one. Display the remaining attributes in bold.
6. Make a copy of the text a double-space below the first.
7. Display all the text in the copy using a Comic Sans MS, 16-point, blue font with regular font style.

Being Responsible
I am responsible when I
. . . arrive at school on time
. . . take pride in my work
. . . cooperate with others
. . . am courteous to others
. . . use my resources wisely
. . . tell the truth
. . . follow instructions
. . . respect others

LESSON 20

Tab

Key each line twice SS (once slowly, then again at a faster pace). DS between 2-line groups.

1 Have my long quiz boxed when Jack stops by for it.
2 when is│are you│you may│they can│where is│to be it
3 Pam may pay the firm for the work they did for us.

PRACTICE MAKES PERFECT

Key each paragraph twice: once slowly, then again at a faster pace. DS between paragraphs. Keep your eyes on the textbook as you strike the *Tab* key.

TECH TALK

The *Tab* key is used to indent the first line of a paragraph. *Typing Time* uses preset or default tabs. The first tab is set 0.5" (5 spaces) to the right of the left margin and is used to indent a paragraph. You will learn to set and clear tabs in a later lesson.

You use the Tabulator key to indent the first line of a paragraph.

Use the same finger you used for keying the A to strike the Tabulator key.

Some letters have all the paragraphs blocked; others, have all the paragraphs indented.

The Tabulator key is often referred to as the Tab key. In fact, most people call it the Tab key.

The Tab key is also used to format columns of numbers. A right tab or a decimal tab is used for numbers.

LESSON 27

Keyboarding Enrichment and Review / and $

CASEY'S WARM UP

Key each line twice SS (once slowly, then again at a faster pace). DS between 2-line groups.

1 Jac likes reviewing problems on the tax quiz on Friday.
2 The order of finish was 92, 234, 82, 165, 170, and 106.
3 If they go to the social, they may visit the six girls.

PRACTICE MAKES PERFECT

Key each line twice SS (once slowly, then again at a faster pace). DS between 2-line groups.

Shift Keys
1 Ann Bob Eve Flo Ida Jon Cara Dawn Gene Helen Kate Larry
2 Ron Uti Yei Zeb Mary Nina Opal Pete Quin Vera Will Xuan
3 Emma Leow | Mena Small | Alexi Pinto | Jack Fuqua | Zena Morrow

Adjacent-Key Words
4 rope post true north grew weight point radio salsa pass
5 error there opens power trade courts renew voices union
6 west crew three lower going import nation thirty trucks

TECHNIQUE TIP

Reach quickly with your little finger to the *Shift* key. Keep your fingers upright and curved.

GRAMMAR CORNER

Read the number usage rule below. Key the Learn line, noting number choices. Key the Apply lines, making the necessary corrections.

Use figures for numbers that follow nouns.

LEARN 1   Read Chapter 12 in Unit 5 for homework.
APPLY 2   Answer Questions four and eight in Chapter five.
APPLY 3   Case 4593 is in Volume three, Section seven.

GRAMMAR CORNER

Read the semicolon rules below. Study the Learn lines. Note how the rules are applied. Compose one sentence (in longhand) for each rule, applying the rule.

Use a semicolon to separate independent clauses in a compound sentence when the conjunction is omitted.

LEARN 1   Doris plays hockey; Delores plays basketball.

LEARN 2   Ted arrived on Friday morning; Alice on Friday evening.

Use a semicolon to separate independent clauses when they are joined by a conjunctive adverb (however, therefore, consequently, and so on).

LEARN 3   Michael lives in Colorado; however, he was born in Wyoming.

LEARN 4   I finished the job on Friday; consequently, I was paid on Monday.

KEYING ON YOUR OWN

Key each line twice SS (slowly, then faster). DS between 2-line groups.

Rows

1   day pop here did sat kept jet got fog like what is
2   ax and man glad came fans zag jab cabs balm Kansas
3   piece price prom web won pin none ice button crept

One-Hand Words

4   pin were look cats joy see you fast limp faded mop
5   at tax sad tea yolk dear union extra milk loop nil
6   As you see, we aced a pop test on a poll tax case.

Balanced-Hand Words

7   of use cut risk for the may half make civic social
8   the big held visit town lake shame girl city vigor
9   Diana may wish to make a formal bid for the signs.

The **font** is the type, or style of letters, in which text is displayed. You can select the font (Times New Roman, Courier New, Arial, Comic Sans MS, etc.) and size you want to use. Size is measured in points. A 12-point font is appropriate for most reports and letters. You can also select the font color.

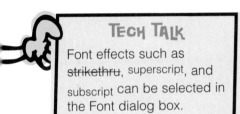

TECH TALK

Font effects such as ~~strikethru~~, superscript, and subscript can be selected in the Font dialog box.

Change Font, Size, and Color

Follow the steps below to change font, size, or color before text is keyed. To change text you have already keyed, select the text and follow the steps below.

1. Click *Format* on the Menu bar. Click *Font*. The Font dialog box appears.
2. Click the font and the size you wish to use. (Use the scroll bars to access more fonts and sizes.)
3. Click the down arrow for the Color drop-down list and click a font color. Click *OK*.

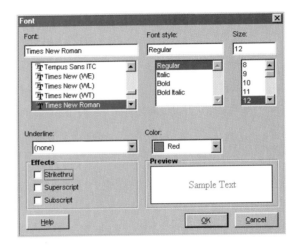

Practice What You Have Learned

1. Key each line using the font, size, and color indicated in the line.

   Key this line using a Times New Roman, blue, 12-point font.
   Key this line using a Comic Sans MS, red, 14-point font.
   Key this line using an Arial, green, 10-point font.
   Key this line using a Courier New, yellow, 12-point font.
   Key this line using a Verdana, black, 18-point font.

2. Change "Key this line" to an Arial, black, 12-point bold font in each line keyed.

© PhotoDisc, Inc.

WRITING CORNER

Compose a paragraph about your favorite holiday. Identify what the holiday celebrates and explain why it is your favorite. Discuss activities or traditions related to the holiday. Save the document as **L26Holiday**.

WRITING CORNER

Lesson 12: **Movie Stars**
Lesson 15: **Inventors**
Lesson 18: **Musicians**

Your teacher will return the paragraphs that you composed for Lessons 12, 15, and 18. Edit the paragraphs, making any additional changes that you wish. Key the paragraphs about each topic in a separate document and save them using the filenames shown at the left. You will use these files for completing a report in Lesson 40.

THINKING CAP

Key each sentence shown at the right. Choose a state capital from the list at the top right to complete each sentence correctly.

Austin   Nashville
Charleston   Phoenix
Denver   Richmond
Dover   Salt Lake City
Montpelier   Santa Fe

The capital of Arizona is _____.

The capital of Colorado is _____.

The capital of New Mexico is _____.

The capital of Texas is _____.

The capital of Utah is _____.

KEYING ON YOUR OWN: REVIEW 0 TO 9

Key each line twice SS (once slowly, then again at a faster pace). DS between 2-line groups.

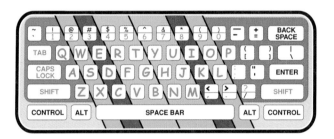

1   Add 17, 28, 39, 45, 30, and 176 to see if 335 is right.

2   Reach quickly when you key 172, 384, 491, 502, and 678.

3   On May 23, 56,047 out of 134,968 people voted for Mike.

4   I practiced keying 12, 34, 56, 78, and 90 very quickly.

5   Sandra subtracted 68 from 139 and 54 from 207 mentally.

SKILL BUILDER 1

SKILL BUILDER Tip

Sentences emphasizing each letter of the alphabet will be keyed in Skill Builders 1–5.

PRACTICE MAKES PERFECT

Key each line twice. Keep your fingers curved and upright.

a   Dana Aaron ate the apple and banana last Saturday.

b   Bo became a better batter by batting rubber balls.

c   Cecilia the raccoon circled the cream colored car.

d   Diana and Don decided to delay their wedding date.

e   Eddie and Eileen decided to leave the event early.

gwam 1' | 1 | 2 | 3 | 4 | 5 | 6 | 7 | 8 | 9 | 10 |

KEYING ON YOUR OWN

Key each line three times: first, to improve keying technique; next, to improve keying speed; last, to build precise control of finger motions. DS between 3-line groups.

SKILL BUILDER Tip

Each of the words used in the drill is among the 600 most-used words in the English language. Practice them frequently to increase your keying speed.

Balanced-Hand Words

1   of to is it he by or an if us so do me am go of it

2   them than also such make then work both down forms

Phrases

3   is it | to me | she may | and own | but due | pay the | of us

4   to end | a big man | make them work | make a wish | own it

Sentences

5   She paid the man for the work he did for the city.

6   She is to pay for half, and he is to pay for half.

Keyboarding Enrichment and Review 0 to 9

CASEY'S WARM UP

Key each line twice SS (once slowly, then again at a faster pace). DS between 2-line groups.

1 Zack Galpow saved the job requirement for the six boys.
2 We sold 134 pizzas, 97 tacos, 206 colas, and 158 chips.
3 If I go to the city to visit them, I may go to the spa.

PRACTICE MAKES PERFECT

Set the Timer for 1 minute. Key at least two 1' timings on each paragraph. Then key two 2' writings on both paragraphs. Determine *gwam* and errors.

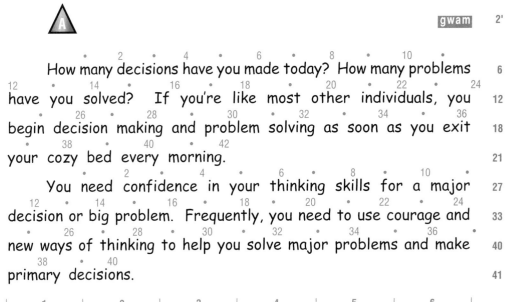

gwam 2'

How many decisions have you made today? How many problems   6
have you solved? If you're like most other individuals, you   12
begin decision making and problem solving as soon as you exit 18
your cozy bed every morning.   21
You need confidence in your thinking skills for a major   27
decision or big problem. Frequently, you need to use courage and 33
new ways of thinking to help you solve major problems and make   40
primary decisions.   41

gwam 2' | 1 | 2 | 3 | 4 | 5 | 6 |

CASEY'S SPEED CHECK

Key each paragraph once SS using word wrap. DS between paragraphs. Set the Timer for 1 minute. Key a 1' timing on each paragraph. Determine *gwam* on each timing. (The figure above the last word keyed is your 1' *gwam*.)

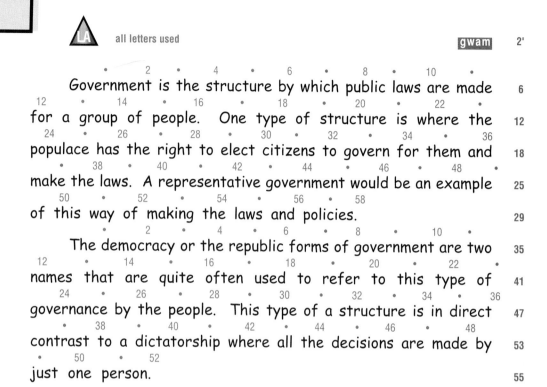

LA   all letters used   gwam   2'

Government is the structure by which public laws are made	6
for a group of people. One type of structure is where the	12
populace has the right to elect citizens to govern for them and	18
make the laws. A representative government would be an example	25
of this way of making the laws and policies.	29
The democracy or the republic forms of government are two	35
names that are quite often used to refer to this type of	41
governance by the people. This type of a structure is in direct	47
contrast to a dictatorship where all the decisions are made by	53
just one person.	55

gwam 2' | 1 | 2 | 3 | 4 | 5 | 6 |

1. Key the lines below.

Get new jeans on Tuesday at the Clothing Factory.

Get a hair cut on Thursday at Hair Loft.

Go to the soccer game on Monday evening at East Field.

Visit Uncle Dan and Aunt Mary on Sunday at Blue Flame Diner.

Pick up Chris and go to social at Holt Jr. High on Friday evening.

Get tickets on Wednesday to go to see Del Tones at Star Arena.

Meet Brett at Happy Times on Saturday.

2. Bold all names of days, italicize all names of people, and underline all names of places.

3. Use Cut/Paste to arrange lines in order by day, starting with Monday.

4. Use Copy/Paste to make two additional copies. Place each copy a quadruple-space below the preceding one.

PRACTICE MAKES PERFECT

Key each line twice. Keep your fingers curved and upright.

f Fred Ford played the fife for his fifteen friends.

g Gregg glanced at the gaggle of geese on the grass.

h When she goes with him, she can help with the ham.

i Ida lived in Illinois, Indiana, and Mississippi.

j Jay Jack Jaha took jeans on the jet to New Jersey.

gwam 1' | 1 | 2 | 3 | 4 | 5 | 6 | 7 | 8 | 9 | 10 |

KEYING ON YOUR OWN

Key each line three times: first, to improve keying technique; next, to improve keying speed; last, to build precise control of finger motions. DS between 3-line groups.

SKILL BUILDER TIP
Each of the words used in the drill is among the 600 most-used words in the English language. Practice them frequently to increase your keying speed.

One-Hand Words

1 in be we on as at no up my you was are him get see

2 war act were only ever face date state great water

Phrases

3 set up | at no | as my | on you | we are | you were | tax case

4 water rate | act on my case | you set a date | free card

Sentences

5 In fact, water rates were only set in state cases.

6 After we get him set on a date, we set a tax rate.

Key each line once. DS between each set of lines.

Practice 2

1 s 2 s 2 s2 s2 ss 22 ss 22 s2s s2s 2s2 2s2 Key 2 and 22.
2 There are 2 of the 22 runners. I just read pages 2-22.

Practice 6

3 j 6 j 6 j6 j6 jj 66 jj 66 j6j j6j 6j6 6j6 Add 6 and 66.
4 Just 6 of 66 have finished. I will pick 6, 66, or 666.

Practice 2 and 6

5 My coach said 22 of the 66 players are 6 minutes early.
6 I can print pages 6 to 22 of Book 2 for the 6 visitors.

WORD PROCESSING
CUT, COPY, AND PASTE

Selected text can be moved or copied to another place. The Cut command removes the selected text from the current location; the Paste command places it in another location. The Copy command copies the selected text so it can be pasted to another location, leaving the original text unchanged.

COMPUTER WIZ

Access the Cut, Copy, and Paste commands quickly by clicking the buttons on the toolbar.

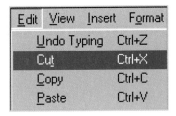

Learn Cut, Copy, and Paste

1. Select the text to be cut or copied.
2. Click *Edit* on the Menu bar. Click *Cut* or *Copy*.
3. To paste text that has been cut or copied, move the insertion point to the desired location.
4. Click *Edit* on the Menu bar. Click *Paste*.

Edit	View	Insert	Format
Undo Typing		Ctrl+Z	
Cut		Ctrl+X	
Copy		Ctrl+C	
Paste		Ctrl+V	

(continued on next page)

Key each paragraph once SS using word wrap. DS between paragraphs. Set the Timer for 1 minute. Key a 1' timing on each paragraph. Determine *gwam* on each timing. (The figure above the last word keyed is your 1' *gwam*.)

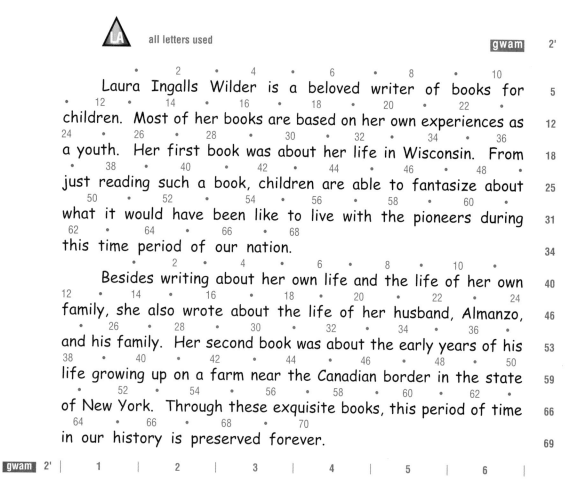

all letters used   gwam   2'

	•	2	•	4	•	6	•	8	•	10		

Laura Ingalls Wilder is a beloved writer of books for   5

children. Most of her books are based on her own experiences as   12

a youth. Her first book was about her life in Wisconsin. From   18

just reading such a book, children are able to fantasize about   25

what it would have been like to live with the pioneers during   31

this time period of our nation.   34

Besides writing about her own life and the life of her own   40

family, she also wrote about the life of her husband, Almanzo,   46

and his family. Her second book was about the early years of his   53

life growing up on a farm near the Canadian border in the state   59

of New York. Through these exquisite books, this period of time   66

in our history is preserved forever.   69

gwam 2' | 1 | 2 | 3 | 4 | 5 | 6 |

LESSON 25

Keyboarding Enrichment and Review 2 and 6

CASEY'S WARM UP

Key each line twice SS (once slowly, then again at a faster pace). DS between 2-line groups.

1 Wei asked Jay for the expensive zoology equipment back.
2 Milers 92, 43, 25, 86, and 107 finished the race first.
3 The man paid a visit to the firm to sign the work form.

ENDURANCE GOAL

When you can key 15–20 *wam* above your 1' *gwam* rate for 15", increase the timings to 30". Move to the next line when you are able to complete at least 2 lines within the 30".

PRACTICE MAKES PERFECT

Set the Timer for 15 seconds. Key at least ten 15" timings, beginning on a line that is approximately 1/4 of your 1' *gwam* rate. Move to the next line when you are able to complete a line within 15". Force your stroking speed to a higher level on each timing.

1 Claudia is to go by auto.
2 I will handle the bus problem.
3 The social may be held by the city.
4 The antique bottle by the shelf is mine.
5 Dixie owns the coalfield that is by the lake.
6 Their neighbor is to go to the big ancient chapel.
7 The field by the cornfield is not good for the bicycle.

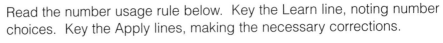

| 15" | 4 | 8 | 12 | 16 | 20 | 24 | 28 | 32 | 36 | 40 | 44 |

CONTROL GOAL

When you can key at 15–20 *wam* above your 1' *gwam* rate for 30", drop back two lines. Try to key that line with not more than one error for 30". Move to the next line when your control goal is met.

GRAMMAR CORNER

Read the number usage rule below. Key the Learn line, noting number choices. Key the Apply lines, making the necessary corrections.

Use figures for house numbers except number One.

LEARN 1 I live at One Ford Drive; Pat lives at 13 Atlas Place.
APPLY 2 He moved from 1 Vero Road to fifteen Rose Drive.
APPLY 3 I drove from 25 Rock Road to 1 Oxford Road.

SKILL BUILDER 3

PRACTICE MAKES PERFECT

Key each line twice. Keep your fingers curved and upright.

k Ken kept Kay's knickknacks in a sack in the kayak.

l Lila filled the small holes in the leftfield wall.

m Mike meets my mom most mornings at the small mall.

n None of those at the noon luncheon knew Nina Lane.

o One of our boys opposed drilling for offshore oil.

gwam 1' | 1 | 2 | 3 | 4 | 5 | 6 | 7 | 8 | 9 | 10 |

KEYING ON YOUR OWN

Key each line three times: first, to improve keying technique; next, to improve keying speed; last, to build precise control of finger motions. DS between 3-line groups.

Double-Letter Words

1 see off all too look been well good need feel will

2 all room keep book bill tell still small free soon

Phrases

3 free room | too soon | need a book | look good | feel good

4 feel free | all week | will soon | small room | soon offer

Sentences

5 They still feel we need a small book for the room.

6 I still feel I need to bill all who call for free.

SKILL BUILDER TIP
Each of the words used in the drill is among the 600 most-used words in the English language. Practice them frequently to increase your keying speed.

Key each line once. DS between each set of lines.

Practice 3

1 d 3 d 3 d3 d3 dd 33 dd 33 d3d d3d 3d3 3d3 Key 3 and 33.

2 Subtract 3 and 33 from 333. The 3 boys have 33 homers.

Practice 0

3 ; 0 ; 0 ;0 ;0 ;; 00 ;; 00 ;0; ;0; 0;0 0;0 Key 0 and 00.

4 Add 0 and 0 to get 0. Do you get number 0, 00, or 000?

Practice 3 and 0

5 Add 3, 30, 33, and 300 and then subtract 33, 30, and 3.

6 I saw 30 hens on my 3 trips to the farm at 333 Hill Dr.

WORD PROCESSING

UNDO AND REDO

Use the Undo . . . command to reverse the last change you made. Undo restores text to its original place, even if you have moved the inser- tion point. Use the Redo . . . command to reverse the last Undo action.

COMPUTER WIZ

Click the *Undo* button on the toolbar to undo an action quickly.

COMPUTER WIZ

To select consecutive words, click at the beginning of the first word. Depress/hold the *Shift* key. Click at the end of the last word.

Learn Undo and Redo

1. Select *Undo* . . . from the Edit menu. Confirm that the desired change was made.

2. If you want to reverse the change, select *Redo* . . . from the Edit menu.

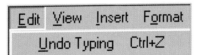   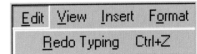

Practice What You Have Learned

1. Key the sentence shown below.

The students of Reed Middle School will perform Cinderella by Charles Perrault on Friday, November 5, in the school auditorium.

2. Bold "Cinderella."

3. Select *Undo Style Change* to reverse the Bold command. Confirm that "Cinderella" is not in bold style.

4. Select *Redo Style Change* to reverse the Undo command. Confirm that "Cinderella" is in bold style.

5. Bold "Friday." Select *Undo Style Change* to reverse the command.

6. Using the method for selecting text described in the Computer Wiz tip, bold "Reed Middle School."

Key each paragraph once SS using word wrap. DS between paragraphs. Set the Timer for 1 minute. Key a 1' timing on each paragraph. Determine *gwam* on each timing. (The figure above the last word keyed is your 1' *gwam*.)

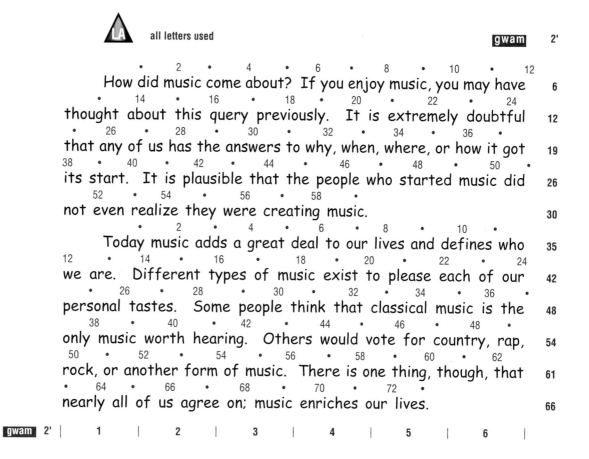

all letters used   gwam   2'

• 2 • 4 • 6 • 8 • 10 • 12	
How did music come about? If you enjoy music, you may have	6
• 14 • 16 • 18 • 20 • 22 • 24	
thought about this query previously. It is extremely doubtful	12
• 26 • 28 • 30 • 32 • 34 • 36 •	
that any of us has the answers to why, when, where, or how it got	19
38 • 40 • 42 • 44 • 46 • 48 • 50 •	
its start. It is plausible that the people who started music did	26
52 • 54 • 56 • 58 •	
not even realize they were creating music.	30
• 2 • 4 • 6 • 8 • 10 •	
Today music adds a great deal to our lives and defines who	35
12 • 14 • 16 • 18 • 20 • 22 • 24	
we are. Different types of music exist to please each of our	42
• 26 • 28 • 30 • 32 • 34 • 36 •	
personal tastes. Some people think that classical music is the	48
38 • 40 • 42 • 44 • 46 • 48 •	
only music worth hearing. Others would vote for country, rap,	54
50 • 52 • 54 • 56 • 58 • 60 • 62	
rock, or another form of music. There is one thing, though, that	61
• 64 • 66 • 68 • 70 • 72 •	
nearly all of us agree on; music enriches our lives.	66

gwam 2' | 1 | 2 | 3 | 4 | 5 | 6 |

LESSON 24

Keyboarding Enrichment and Review 3 and 0

CASEY'S WARM UP

Key each line twice SS (once slowly, then again at a faster pace). DS between 2-line groups.

1 Jim quickly realized the beautiful gowns are expensive.
2 Janet said 418 of my 597 classmates scored at least 30.
3 Pamela may go visit them by the cornfield and big lake.

PRACTICE MAKES PERFECT

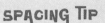

TECHNIQUE GOAL
Use a quick, down-and-in thumb motion. Keep your fingers upright and curved.

SPACING TIP
No space is left before or after : when used with figures to express time. Key **a.m.** and **p.m.** without spaces between the letters and periods.

Key each line twice SS (once slowly, then again at a faster pace). DS between 2-line groups.

Space Bar
1 if she|or she|he may|it can|she ran|it will be|give the
2 His wish is to see the sun set over the water each day.
3 I saw the new red car with blue top come up the street.

Adjacent-Key Words
4 are err has sap ion oil wet new try pod opt quiz medium
5 ads tire very past said riot join went view part weekly
6 score other waste sales union moist weaves renews birth

GRAMMAR CORNER

Read the number usage rule below. Key the Learn line, noting number choices. Key the Apply lines, making the necessary corrections.

Use figures to express time.

LEARN 1 My flight will land at 7:55 p.m.
APPLY 2 This class meets from nine ten to ten ten a.m.
APPLY 3 Practice begins at three thirty five p.m.

SKILL BUILDER 4

PRACTICE MAKES PERFECT

Key each line twice. Keep your fingers curved and upright.

p   The playful puppies pulled the paper wrapping off.

q   Quincy quickly quit questioning the quiet quartet.

r   Rupert arrived after a car ride on the rural road.

s   Susan sat still as soon as she saw the sushi dish.

t   Ted left the tater tots on top of the counter top.

gwam 1' | 1 | 2 | 3 | 4 | 5 | 6 | 7 | 8 | 9 | 10 |

KEYING ON YOUR OWN

Key each line three times: first, to improve keying technique; next, to improve keying speed; last, to build precise control of finger motions. DS between 3-line groups.

Word Response

1   The maid paid the man to fix the auto turn signal.

2   Diana is to handle all the pay forms for the city.

3   The girls cut their hair when they go to the city.

4   Keith may be the right man to blame for the fight.

5   Kay may wish to pay for the sign for the neighbor.

6   I may also wish to make a formal bid for the auto.

You can italicize, **bold (darken),** *and* <u>underline</u> *existing text by using the same buttons or pull-down menu as you did in Lesson 22.*

COMPUTER WIZ

To select a word quickly and easily, place the insertion point within the word and double-click.

Apply Italic, Bold, and Underline to Existing Text

1. Select (highlight) the text to be formatted.

2. Click *Format* on the Menu bar. Click *Font*. The Font dialog box appears.

3. Click the desired formatting for Font style. Click the down arrow for the Underline drop-down list box to select an underline style. Click *OK*.

Practice What You Have Learned

1. Key the paragraph below.

   Tom Holt from Ford Middle School scored 174, Mary Quinonnes from Evans City Junior High scored 182, and Lin Lon from Thompson Middle School scored 188. Jen Holt-Olsen from Cerritos Middle School won first place with a score of 198.

2. Bold the names of the people, italicize the names of the schools, and underline the scores.

© PhotoDisc, Inc.

WRITING CORNER

Search the Internet (or other reference sources) to learn about the month, day, and year (e.g., July 22, 1988) of your birth. Identify two or three significant events for that day and compose a paragraph that identifies and describes the events. Save the document as **L23Date**.

CASEY'S SPEED CHECK

Key each paragraph once SS using word wrap. DS between paragraphs. Set the Timer for 1 minute. Key a 1' timing on each paragraph. Determine *gwam* on each timing. (The figure above the last word keyed is your 1' *gwam*.)

A all letters used

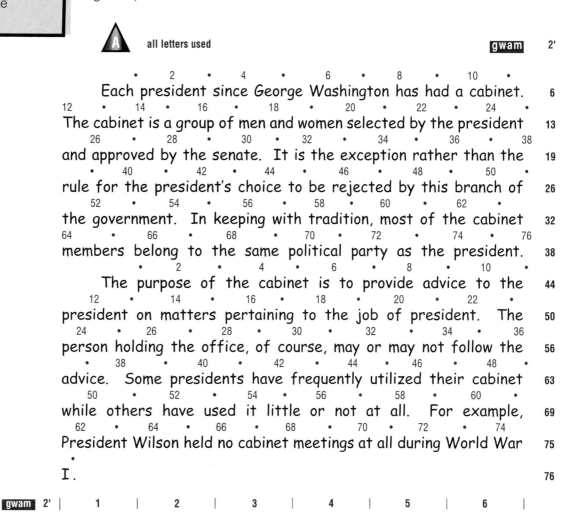

	gwam 2'
• 2 • 4 • 6 • 8 • 10 •	
Each president since George Washington has had a cabinet.	6
12 • 14 • 16 • 18 • 20 • 22 • 24 •	
The cabinet is a group of men and women selected by the president	13
26 • 28 • 30 • 32 • 34 • 36 • 38	
and approved by the senate. It is the exception rather than the	19
• 40 • 42 • 44 • 46 • 48 • 50 •	
rule for the president's choice to be rejected by this branch of	26
52 • 54 • 56 • 58 • 60 • 62 •	
the government. In keeping with tradition, most of the cabinet	32
64 • 66 • 68 • 70 • 72 • 74 • 76	
members belong to the same political party as the president.	38
• 2 • 4 • 6 • 8 • 10 •	
The purpose of the cabinet is to provide advice to the	44
12 • 14 • 16 • 18 • 20 • 22 •	
president on matters pertaining to the job of president. The	50
24 • 26 • 28 • 30 • 32 • 34 • 36	
person holding the office, of course, may or may not follow the	56
• 38 • 40 • 42 • 44 • 46 • 48 •	
advice. Some presidents have frequently utilized their cabinet	63
50 • 52 • 54 • 56 • 58 • 60 •	
while others have used it little or not at all. For example,	69
62 • 64 • 66 • 68 • 70 • 72 • 74	
President Wilson held no cabinet meetings at all during World War	75
•	
I.	76

gwam 2' | 1 | 2 | 3 | 4 | 5 | 6 |

Read the number usage rule below. Key the Learn line, noting number choices. Key the Apply lines, making the necessary corrections.

Use figures to express a day of the month following the month name.

LEARN 1   Sue said she can arrive on January 14.
APPLY 2   The game will be played on May six.
APPLY 3   School begins on September third.

KEYING ON YOUR OWN: REVIEW 5 AND 9

Key each line once. DS between each set of lines.

Practice 5

1   f 5 f 5 f5 f5 ff 55 ff 55 f5f f5f 5f5 5f5 Key 5 and 55.

2   Quickly key 5, 55, and 555. Her age is 55 plus 5 and 5.

Practice 9

3   l 9 l 9 l9 l9 ll 99 ll 99 l9l l9l 9l9 9l9 Key 9 and 99.

4   I will add 9, 99, and 999. Subtract 9 and 99 from 999.

Practice 5 and 9

5   Add 5, 9, 55, 59, 95, and 99. Eric hit 5 of 9 targets.

6   Tom and the 5 starters scored 55 of the 99 game points.

SKILL BUILDER 5

PRACTICE MAKES PERFECT

Key each line twice. Keep your fingers curved and upright.

u Ursula usually rushes up to see us unload the bus.

v Vivian voted to view the very vivid travel videos.

w Wes Weston waved wildly when he saw the two wrens.

x Six tax experts explored the extreme tax expenses.

y Mary Yount saw the Yankees play in New York City.

z Zachary was puzzled by the zigzag zipper stitches.

`gwam` 1' | 1 | 2 | 3 | 4 | 5 | 6 | 7 | 8 | 9 | 10 |

KEYING ON YOUR OWN

Key each line three times: first, to improve keying technique; next to improve keying speed; last, to build precise control of finger motions. DS between 3-line groups.

Word Response

1 Vivian is to pay the six firms for all their work.

2 Eight of the girls may go to the city by the lake.

3 They may make a bicycle lane for them by the lake.

4 A proficient maid may shake the rug for the girls.

5 A big man is with the dog by the sign to the lake.

6 If they wish me to do so, I may go to the auditor.

Keyboarding Enrichment and Review 5 and 9

CASEY'S WARM UP

Key each line twice SS (once slowly, then again at a faster pace). DS between 2-line groups.

1 Bajif was amazingly quick during the extensive program.
2 He practiced keying 1, 57, 748, and 1,959 very quickly.
3 The girls may pay for the big emblem with their profit.

PRACTICE MAKES PERFECT

Set the Timer for 1 minute. Key at least two 1' timings on each paragraph. Then key two 2' timings on both paragraphs. Determine *gwam* and errors.

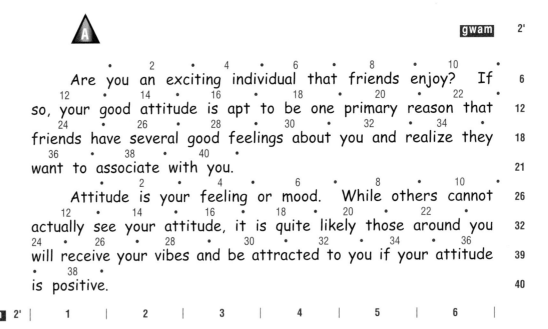

	gwam	2'

Are you an exciting individual that friends enjoy? If 6
so, your good attitude is apt to be one primary reason that 12
friends have several good feelings about you and realize they 18
want to associate with you. 21

Attitude is your feeling or mood. While others cannot 26
actually see your attitude, it is quite likely those around you 32
will receive your vibes and be attracted to you if your attitude 39
is positive. 40

gwam 2' | 1 | 2 | 3 | 4 | 5 | 6 |

CASEY'S SPEED CHECK

Key each paragraph once SS using word wrap. DS between paragraphs. Set the Timer for 1 minute. Key a 1' timing on each paragraph. Determine *gwam* on each timing. (The figure above the last word keyed is your 1' *gwam*.)

A all letters used

| | gwam | 2' |

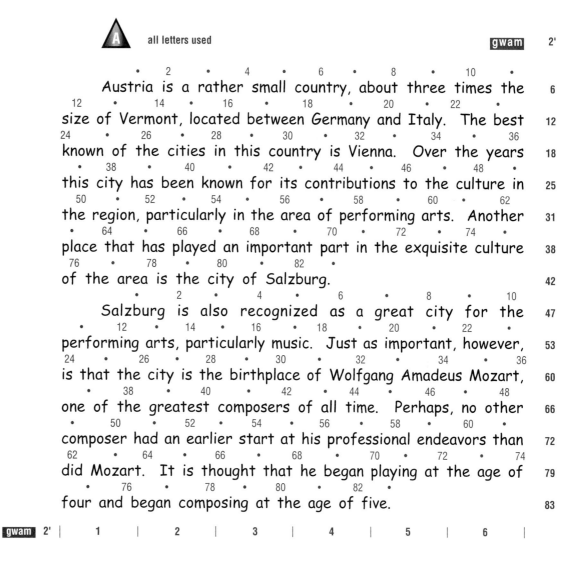

	gwam
• 2 • 4 • 6 • 8 • 10 • Austria is a rather small country, about three times the	6
12 • 14 • 16 • 18 • 20 • 22 • size of Vermont, located between Germany and Italy. The best	12
24 • 26 • 28 • 30 • 32 • 34 • 36 known of the cities in this country is Vienna. Over the years	18
• 38 • 40 • 42 • 44 • 46 • 48 • this city has been known for its contributions to the culture in	25
50 • 52 • 54 • 56 • 58 • 60 • 62 the region, particularly in the area of performing arts. Another	31
• 64 • 66 • 68 • 70 • 72 • 74 • place that has played an important part in the exquisite culture	38
76 • 78 • 80 • 82 • of the area is the city of Salzburg.	42
• 2 • 4 • 6 • 8 • 10 Salzburg is also recognized as a great city for the	47
• 12 • 14 • 16 • 18 • 20 • 22 • performing arts, particularly music. Just as important, however,	53
24 • 26 • 28 • 30 • 32 • 34 • 36 is that the city is the birthplace of Wolfgang Amadeus Mozart,	60
• 38 • 40 • 42 • 44 • 46 • 48 • one of the greatest composers of all time. Perhaps, no other	66
• 50 • 52 • 54 • 56 • 58 • 60 • composer had an earlier start at his professional endeavors than	72
62 • 64 • 66 • 68 • 70 • 72 • 74 did Mozart. It is thought that he began playing at the age of	79
• 76 • 78 • 80 • 82 • four and began composing at the age of five.	83

gwam 2' | 1 | 2 | 3 | 4 | 5 | 6 |

3. Key the text. To resume keying with regular character style, access the Font dialog box. Select *Regular* for Font style and *(none)* for Underline.

Practice What You Have Learned

Bold, italicize, and underline text as shown as you key the copy below.

Tim used the **bold** feature to see the **main points** in his notes.

Italic or <u>underline</u> is acceptable for book titles.

Shakespeare wrote *Hamlet* and *Much Ado About Nothing*.

Do you know the difference between <u>principal</u> and <u>principle</u>?

This sentence has **bold**, *italic*, and <u>underlined</u> letters.

Use ***bold***, ***italics***, and <u>***underlining***</u> on the same word sparingly.

Keyboarding Enrichment and Review 1 and 7

CASEY'S WARM UP

Key each line twice SS (once slowly, then again at a faster pace). DS between 2-line groups.

1 Jany gave Hobi an exquisite prize, a framed wall clock.
2 I asked for 7 not 11. I have 7 of the 11 songs played.
3 She may sign a proxy if they make an audit of the firm.

PRACTICE MAKES PERFECT

Key each line twice SS (once slowly, then again at a faster pace). DS between 2-line groups.

TECHNIQUE TIP

Keep your fingers upright and curved. Use quick-snap strokes and keep your eyes on the copy.

Home/Upper-Row Reaches

1 it of we us if up to hi two raw pop pit put you far her
2 wet pop you tot pep got kit lot hit deal hold quit quay
3 two four pour eight quiet joust quote twilight yourself

Consecutive-Direct Reaches

4 many much loan side grow golf price delay checks manual
5 thus wide gift slow gold fund owned album chance turned
6 enemy hence forum demand signed length bright editorial

GRAMMAR CORNER

Read the number usage rule below. Key the Learn line, noting number choices. Key the Apply lines, making the necessary corrections.

Spell a number that begins a sentence even when other numbers in the sentence are shown in figures.

LEARN 1   Seven girls got a total of 16 hits and 11 runs.
APPLY 2   20 boys collected 52 toys today and 29 yesterday.
APPLY 3   12 skaters, 14 skiers, and 16 jumpers went on the trip.

Key each line once. DS between each set of lines.

Practice 4

1   f 4 f 4 f4 f4 ff 44 ff 44 f4f f4f 4f4 4f4 Key 4 and 44.

2   She saw 4 cows and 14 hens. I will read pages 4 to 44.

Practice 8

3   k 8 k 8 k8 k8 kk 88 kk 88 k8k k8k 8k8 8k8 Key 8 and 88.

4   Divide 88 by 8 and 888 by 88. Sara missed 8 out of 88.

Practice 4 and 8

5   Add 4, 44, 8, 88, and 48. Just 8 of 88 racers stopped.

6   Reach quickly when you key 4, 8, 44, 88, 444, and 8844.

WORD PROCESSING

BOLD, ITALIC, AND UNDERLINE

*Use formatting commands to create italic letters, **bold (dark) text**, and underline text as you key. You will learn about other options in the Font dialog box in a later lesson.*

COMPUTER WIZ

Click the *Bold, Italic,* and *Underline* buttons on the toolbar to set format options quickly.

Apply Italic, Bold, and Underline as You Key

1.   Click *Format* on the Menu bar. Click *Font*. The Font dialog box appears.

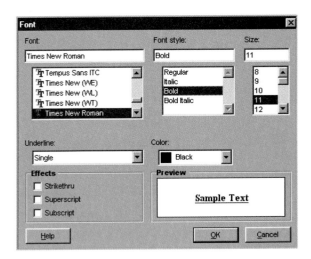

2.   Click the desired formatting for Font style. Click the down arrow for the Underline drop-down list box to select an underline style. Click *OK*.

(continued on next page)

Key each line once. DS between each set of lines.

Practice 1

1 a 1 a 1 a1 a1 aa 11 aa 11 a1a a1a 1a1 1a1 Key 1 and 11.

2 Reach to 1, 11, 111. Go to page 1 in Chapter 11 on 1/1.

Practice 7

3 j 7 j 7 j7 j7 jj 77 jj 77 j7j j7j 7j7 7j7 Key 7 and 77.

4 Can you add 7, 77, and 777? Did the 7 boys eat 7 pies?

Practice 1 and 7

5 Add 1, 7, 11, 17, 71, and 77. I saw 17 of the 71 plays.

6 The racer wanted number 77 but had to choose 17 or 717.

WORD PROCESSING

REVIEW WORD PROCESSOR SCREEN

As shown at the right, the Word Processor has a Menu bar, a toolbar, and a Ruler. You can use the commands and options on the Menu bar, toolbar, and Ruler to format and change what you key.

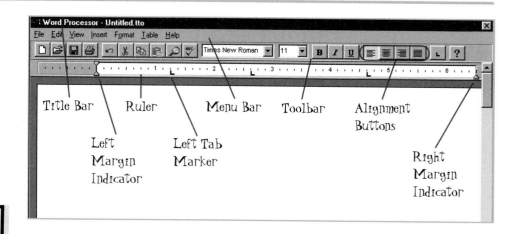

TECH TALK

Menu Bar: Contains commands in seven pull-down menus.

Toolbar: Contains buttons used for quick access to frequently used commands.

Ruler: Shows margin and tab settings.

Preview WP Commands

1. Click on each of the seven menus on the Menu bar and read the list of commands and options on each pull-down menu. Which commands and options have you used in previous lessons?

2. Point to each button on the toolbar to identify the command the button represents. Can you access these commands via the pull-down menus?

3. Identify the Tab Type and Alignment buttons on the Ruler. How many alignment styles can you use?

CASEY'S WARM UP

Key each line twice SS (once slowly, then again at a faster pace). DS between 2-line groups.

1 Zelda might soon fix the job growth plans very quickly.
2 On May 14, 4,718 voters will cast votes for 18 offices.
3 Pamela and Kay may fix the penalty box when they visit.

PRACTICE MAKES PERFECT

Set the Timer for 15 seconds. Key at least ten 15" timings, beginning on a line that is approximately 1/4 of your 1' *gwam* rate. Move to the next line when you are able to complete a line within 15". Force your stroking speed to a higher level on each timing.

1 Jane is to key the audit.
2 I may suspend the men in town.
3 Make the title forms for the firms.
4 The woman paid the girl to fix the sign.
5 Ellen may bid on the antique chair and rifle.
6 Che kept the men down at the big lake by the city.
7 Claudia may go with us to the city to pay for the coal.

15" | 4 | 8 | 12 | 16 | 20 | 24 | 28 | 32 | 36 | 40 | 44 |

ENDURANCE GOAL

When you can key 15–20 *wam* above your 1' *gwam* rate for 15", increase the timings to 30". Move to the next line when you are able to complete at least 2 lines within the 30".

CONTROL GOAL

When you can key at 15–20 *wam* above your 1' *gwam* rate for 30", drop back two lines. Try to key that line with not more than one error for 30". Move to the next line when your control goal is met.

GRAMMAR CORNER

Read the number usage rule below. Key the Learn line, noting number choices. Key the Apply lines, making the necessary corrections.

Use figures for numbers above ten, and for numbers one through ten when they are used with numbers above ten.

LEARN 1   He asked for 8 hot dogs, 12 sodas, and 10 fries.
APPLY 2   I missed eight of fifty-five exam questions.
APPLY 3   Harry was absent three days of the last fifteen days.

INDEX

0 key, control of, 66–67
1 key, control of, 58–59
2 key, control of, 68–69
3 key, control of, 66–67
4 key, control of, 60–61
5 key, control of, 63–64
6 key, control of, 68–69
7 key, control of, 58–59
8 key, control of, 60–61
9 key, control of, 63–64

A

A key, control of, 2, 4, 5, 48
Accept/except, 113
Adjacent-key words, 66, 74
Affect/effect, 118
Align Center button, 78
Align Left button, 78
Align Right button, 78
Alignment, paragraph, 77–78
Alignment buttons, 59
Ampersand key, control of, 80
Apostrophe key, control of, 86
Asterisk key, control of, 89
At sign key, control of, 92
Avenues, streets, and roads, capitalization rules, 18

B

B key, control of, 26–27, 48
Backslash key, control of, 96
Backspace key, 21
Balanced-hand words, 48
Bold attribute, 61–62
Bracket keys, control of, 99
Buy/by, 9

C

C key, control of, 17–18, 48
Capital letters, keying, 23
Capitalization rules: cities, states, and countries, 11; days of week, 11; first word of sentence, 4; historic periods and events, 18; holiday names, 18; months of year, 11; names of people, 4; nouns preceding numbers, 76; personal titles, 4; streets, roads, and avenues, 18
CAPS LOCK key, control of, 42–43

Center alignment, 77
Center tabs, 87
Cities, capitalization rules for, 11
Close button, 3
Codes, showing and hiding, 110
Colon: spacing after, 40; spacing with when expressing time, 66
Colon key, control of, 40–41
Comma, rules for, 32, 39
Comma key, control of, 35–36
Consecutive-direct reaches, 58
Copy button, 69
Copy command, 69–70
Corrections, using Backspace and Delete keys to make, 21
Countries, capitalization rules for, 11
Cut button, 69
Cut command, 69–70

D

D key, control of, 2, 4, 5, 48
Date button, 105
Days of week, capitalization rules for, 11
Decimal tabs, 87
Delete key, 21
Diagonal key, control of, 75
Divide key, control of, 75
Document: opening, 5; printing, 11; saving, 3, 6; saving with new name, 5
Dollar sign key, control of, 75
Double-letter words, 52, 91

E

E key, control of, 6–7, 48
Effect/affect, 118
Ellipsis, 75
Enter/Return key, to insert space, 2
Equals sign key, control of, 99
Except/accept, 113
Exclamation point, 25
Exclamation point key, control of, 96

F

F key, control of, 2, 4, 5, 50
First line indent, 94
First-row keys, 25
First/third-row keys, 18, 34
Font, 61, 73
Font color, 73

Font effects, 73
Font size, 73
For/four, 36
Formatting buttons, 61
Formatting commands, 61
Four/for, 36

G

G key, control of, 24–25, 50
Greater than key, control of, 102
gwam, finding, 43

H

H key, control of, 6–7, 50
Hanging indent, 94
Hard page breaks, 102–103
Headers, 105; multiple, 106; page number in, 105–106
Hear/here, 16
Historic periods and events, capitalization rules, 18
Holiday names, capitalization rules, 18
Home/first-row keys, 91
Home keys, 1–2, 4–5, 8
Home/upper-row reaches, 58
Hour/our, 23
Hyphen key, control of, 77

I

I key, control of, 12–13, 50
Insertion point, moving, 15
Italic attribute, 61–62
Its/it's, 2

J

J key, control of, 2, 4, 5, 50
Justified alignment, 77
Justify button, 78

K

K key, control of, 2, 4, 5, 52
Knew/new, 101
Know/no, 30

L

L key, control of, 2, 4, 5, 52
Left alignment, 77

**Left-hand words, 82, 101
Left margin indicator, 59
Left Shift key, control of, 14-15
Left tab marker, 59
Left tabs, 87
Less than key, control of, 102
Line spacing, 2
Line spacing command, 81
Loan/lone, 104

M
M key, control of, 31-32, 52
Margins, setting, 92-93
Menu bar, 3, 59
**Minus sign key, control of, 77
Months, capitalization rules for, 11
Mouse, using to move insertion point, 15
**Multiply key, control of, 89

N
N key, control of, 22-23, 52
Names of people, capitalization rules, 4
New command, 5
New/knew, 101
No/know, 30
Number keys, 58-73
Number of Pages button, 105
**Number (pound sign) key, control of, 80
Number usage rules, spelling out versus figures, 58, 60, 64, 66, 68, 72, 74, 76, 80, 83, 86

O
O key, control of, 8-9, 52
One-hand words, 50
One/won, 95
Open button, 5
Open command, 5
Our/hour, 23

P
P key, control of, 26-27, 54
Page breaks, 102-103
Page indicator, 103
Page number, in header, 105-106
Page Number button, 105
Paragraph alignment, 77-78
Paragraph indents, setting, 94
Paragraphs, indenting, 45
**Parentheses keys, control of, 83
Paste button, 69
Paste command, 69-70
**Percent key, control of, 77
**Period key, control of, 14-15
Periods, 25; spacing after, 14; spacing in a.m. and p.m., 66
Personal titles, capitalization rules, 4
**Plus sign key, control of, 92
**Pound sign key, control of, 80

Print button, 11
Print command, 11
Print dialog box, 113
Printing: a document, 11; selected pages, 113-114
Proofreaders' marks, 105, 110, 113
Pull-down menu, 3
Punctuation marks: comma, 32, 39; exclamation point, 25; period, 25; question mark, 25; semicolon, 46; colon, 40; spacing after period, 14; spacing after question mark, 42; spacing after semicolon, 6

Q
Q key, control of, 35-36, 54
Question mark, 25; spacing after, 42
**Question mark key, control of, 42-43
**Quotation mark key, control of, 86
Quotations, formatting long, 116

R
R key, control of, 8-9, 54
Redo command, 67
Reports: creating title page for, 111; formatting short, 107-108; textual citations and references in, 114; two-page with textual citations and references, 116-117
Right-hand words, 101
Right margin indicator, 59
**Right Shift key, control of, 24-25
Right tabs, 87
Roads, streets, and avenues, capitalization rules, 18
Ruler, 59; changing side margins using, 93; clearing tabs using, 90

S
S key, control of, 2, 4, 5, 54
Save As command, 5
Save button, 3, 6
Save command, 3
Saving a document, 3, 6; with new name, 5
Selecting a word, 65
Selecting consecutive words, 67
**Semicolon: rules for, 46; spacing after, 6
**Semicolon key, control of, 2, 4, 5
Sentences, capitalization rules, 4
Series, use of comma in, 32
Shift-CAPS LOCK, 82
**Shift keys, 23, 30, 74
**Slash key, control of, 75
Soft page breaks, 102
Space bar, 13, 30, 34, 66
Spacing: after colon, 40; after period, 14; after semicolons, 6; line 2; parentheses and, 83

Speed checks, 49, 51, 53, 55, 57
Spell Check, 96-97
Spell Check button, 96
Standard word, 29
States, capitalization rules for, 11
Streets, roads, and avenues, capitalization rules, 18

T
T key, control of, 12-13, 54
**Tab key, control of, 45-46
Tab Style button, 87
Tabs: clearing, 90; setting, 87
Textual citations and references, 114
Third-row keys, 10, 13, 15, 25, 27
Timed writings, 51, 53, 55, 57, 60, 63, 68, 71, 76, 79, 85, 88, 95, 98, 104, 109, 112, 115
Timer button, 28
Timer dialog box, 28-29
Timer feature, 28-29
Title bar, 3, 59
Title page, 111
To/too/two, 89
Toolbar, 3, 59
Two/to/too, 89

U
U key, control of, 17-18, 56
Underline attribute, 61-62
**Underline key, control of, 89
Undo button, 67
Undo command, 67

V
V key, control of, 40-41, 56

W
W key, control of, 22-23, 56
Wait/weight, 99
Weight/wait, 99
Won/one, 95
Word Processor: accessing, 1; exiting, 3
Word processor command, previewing, 59
Word wrap, 37

X
X key, control of, 31-32, 56

Y
Y key, control of, 33-34, 56
Your/you're, 43

Z
Z key, control of, 33-34, 56